How you doin'?!

Al [signature]

Praise for
The StreetSavvy Leader

"Al Lucia is not afraid to tackle any subject he believes is going to add to your bottom line. He has the unique ability to take what others make complex and confusing, and break it down into simple terms that just about anyone can implement."

    Jason Sage
    Americas Regional Center Manager, Caterpillar

"*The StreetSavvy Leader* shares powerful leadership lessons for the workplace and some great life lessons as well. It creatively ties leadership skills to childhood stories to make the lessons both relatable and memorable, and encourages the reader to conjure up and learn from their own life experiences."

    Charlyn Jarrells Porter
    Retired Chief Diversity Officer and Senior Vice President, Wal-Mart

"You've nailed it! A common sense, practical and effective approach to leadership. More than just theory, leaders at all levels can take this advice and turn it into results."

    Kipp Sassaman
    Vice President of Human Resources, Christopher & Banks

"Great leaders have an edge – the ability to do what needs to be done, even when it isn't popular or comfortable. Al makes you look in the mirror and ask yourself the hard questions. *The StreetSavvy Leader* offers real-world insights into real-world issues without all the rhetoric."

>Steve DerManuelian
>Vice President of Field Human Resources, OfficeMax

"The StreetSavvy concept is to leadership what K.I.S.S. is to management."

>Bob Browning
>Former Regional Human Resources Director,
>American Red Cross

"*The StreetSavvy Leader* has struck a chord with me and brought back a ton of memories from my Philadelphia days. It is loaded with leadership advice and great examples."

>Pat Williams
>Senior Vice President, Orlando Magic

"Al has done a masterful job relating his childhood memories in South Philly to the timeless leadership principles he has been teaching for years. These principles have served me well over the years and have been the cornerstones of the leadership programs I've implemented in the organizations in which I've served. There is nothing like the simplicity of tried and true leadership lessons."

>Sean Burke
>Vice President of Human Resources, American Water

"Like so many of Al Lucia's books and articles, *The StreetSavvy Leader* cuts to the heart of the matter and provides real-world solutions that can be applied in today's businesses."

    Pat Jannausch
    Vice President of Culture & Training, Con-Way Transportation

"Holy cheesesteak! Al Lucia has done it again with his latest gem, *The Street Savvy Leader* – a book that is both can't-put-it-down entertaining and jam-packed with leadership 'life lessons' for us all."

    Eric Harvey
    Best-selling Author, *WALK THE TALK...And Get the Results You Want* and *Ethics4Everyone*

"*The StreetSavvy Leader* is a witty and entertaining easy-read, but also a no-nonsense guide to improved leadership at all levels. In plain language, Al exposes leadership issues and then discusses practical ways to improve."

    Jim Stanfield
    General Manager, Lakeland Electric

"Al's new – and perhaps best – book is consistent with the way he lives, speaks and consults…straightforward, effective and delivered with the right combination of candor and sensitivity."

    Russell Beard
    Director of Staffing, Public Storage

Other Books Authored or Co-authored by Al Lucia:

144 Ways to Walk the Talk

A Slice of Life: A Story about Perspective, Priorities and Pizza

Back to Basics: Tried and True Solutions for Today's Leaders

Employee Commitment: If You Build It, Results Will Come

JukeBox Journey to Success

Rock Your Way to Happiness: Harmogenize, a Fun Way to a More Fulfilling Life

The Leadership Secrets of Santa Claus

Walk the Talk…And Get the Results You Want

Walking the Talk Together: Sharing the Responsibility for Bringing Values to Life

THE STREETSAVVY LEADER

Get Real. Get Results.

by Al Lucia

Copyright © 2010 Al Lucia. All rights reserved.

No part of this book may be reproduced or transmitted in any form or by any means, electronic or mechanical, including photocopying, recording, or by an information storage and retrieval system – except by a reviewer who may quote brief passages in a review to be printed in a magazine or newspaper – without written permission in advance from the publisher. International rights and foreign translations available only through negotiation with the publisher.

Inquiries regarding permission for use of the material contained in this book should be addressed to:
    Jukebox Publishing Group
    1111 Holy Grail
    Lewisville, TX 75056
    (972) 662-3068

Although the author and publisher have made every effort to ensure the accuracy and completeness of information contained in this book, we assume no responsibility for errors, inaccuracies, omissions, or any inconsistency herein. Any slights of people, places or organizations are unintentional.

Printed in the United States of America
ISBN: 978-0-9669099-1-3

Credits

Collaborating Editor:
    Juli Baldwin
    The Baldwin Group, Dallas, TX
    Juli@BaldwinGrp.com

Cover Design:
    Melissa Monogue
    Back Porch Creative, Plano, TX
    info@BackPorchCreative.com

Interior Design and Layout:
    Katie Booth
    katie@katiebooth.com

To Marion and Al Lucia…

Two people who knew what the word "parent" meant and who gave me indelible values, examples and lessons that guide me and help me to this day.

*My parents – Marion and Al Lucia –
strolling the boardwalk in Atlantic City, NJ, in 1942.*

Contents

How *You* Doin'? 1

How *"Youse"* Can Best *Use* This Book 7

1. Call "Chips on the Ball"…
   Hold Others – and Yourself – Accountable for Results 9

2. "Look! It's a Bird! It's a Plane! It's Superman!"…
   **Discover the Superhuman Power of
   Comic Book Communication** 21

3. Say "Hunks!"…
   Use Unwritten Rules to Get More of What You Want 31

4. Stop the Broad Street Bullies…
   Start with Yourself 39

5. Let 'Em Know How *They* are Doin'…
   Deliver Painless Performance Appraisal 49

6. "Climb in My Window"…
   Leverage Generational Strengths 59

7. Utilize Street Specialists…
   Practice "Right Fit" Leadership 69

8. Take a Tip From the Butcher Shop Ladies…
   Use the Power of Influence 79

9. Join a Gang…
   Model Your Employer Brand 87

10. Honor "La Famiglia"…
    Respect Your Team Enough to Empower It 97

11. Live in the City of Brotherly Love…
    Stop the Recognition Paradox 109

12. Scrub Your Steps…
    Polish Your Organizational Pride 119

13. Play Halfball and Dead Box…
    Get Creative and Have Some Fun 127

14. "Roof It"…
    Select the Top Priorities and Get Rid of the Rest 137

15. Set Your Beach Chair on the Sidewalk…
    Commit to Work-Life Balance 147

16. Cheer for the Pomacs…
    Coach Your Way to Success 157

17. Check Out the New Kid on the Block…
    Address Cultural Fit Problems Early 171

18. Trade Your Rags for Pots and Pans…
    Swap Your Old "Stuff" for Something Better 179

19. Change "The Way You Do the Things You Do"…
    Get Bigger Returns for the Same Investment of Time 189

20. Fight City Hall…
    Hold Leaders Accountable All the Way Down the Line 199

21. Remember Uncle Tony's Cigar Box…
    Sweat the Small Stuff 207

Yo! So Now You Think You Know Everything? 215

StreetSavvy Glossary 219

Acknowledgements 225

About the Author 226

How *You* Doin'?

Let's get real…

You are well aware of the challenges you face every day as a leader. You read the popular leadership books and blogs. You attend the leadership-development conferences, workshops and seminars. You know what you need to do to be successful as a leader:

- Hold employees accountable for results;
- Deal with four generations in the workplace;
- Attract, retain and manage your talent;
- Juggle many, often-conflicting "top priorities";
- Deliver better-than-ever customer service from the same employees whom you're asking to do more and more with less and less;
- Handle tough performance problems;
- Engage staff members who do just enough to get by;
- Manage never-ending change – not only for your team, but also for yourself;
- Meet increasing demand by shareholders for a healthy return on investment.

So let me ask you: *When it comes to your role as a leader, how you doin'?*

Really…how you doin'?

My bet is, if you're totally honest with yourself, you're still having a tough time. You likely know what to do. It's the *doing* part that's the challenge.

I can relate. Having been a leader myself, I know that you want proven, practical solutions that work in the real world. And having worked with leaders at all levels – in organizations ranging from Fortune 100 global conglomerates to small businesses – I know that conventional leadership advice isn't working for most leaders.

Too often, leadership experts give conceptual solutions, leaving you no more effective than you were before you read the book or attended the latest-rage workshop. Or they offer specific techniques and strategies that aren't practical to use in the real world when it's 3:00 on a Thursday and you're in the middle of a crisis or dealing with employees who aren't doing their job (again!).

I'm telling you right now, you won't find theories, fads or some management "flavor of the month" here. What you will find in this book are actionable strategies, practical tools and step-by-step techniques to resolve your everyday challenges rather than avoid them, dance around them or procrastinate on them.

I'm going to tell it like it is, say what others won't say and get real about what goes on inside organizations, knowing full well that I might upset some people. I don't tiptoe around the issues, and I don't mince words. Why? Because I'm from South Philly (a colorful neighborhood in Philadelphia, Pennsylvania) and that's the way we do it there.

South Philly was a great place to grow up. I'm often reminded of the sights, sounds, smells and experiences of my youth: kids hanging out on the street corner for hours on end…the street vendor calling "Hot waffles!"…the smell of a fresh cheesesteak… the feel of a Halfball in my hand…and my tastiest memory, Mom's gravy (Italians never call it sauce.)

Of course, it wasn't Utopia. The streets of South Philly have always been rough. We certainly had our share of hardships, unpleasant situations, bad influences and provincial attitudes. As a kid, I learned quickly that you had to be street savvy to get by. You had to be clear about who you were, what you stood for… and what you *wouldn't* stand for. We knew what was important. We were practical – there was no time for B.S. and no money to waste. We did what we had to do to get things done; to make things happen. The people in our neighborhood were authentic and forthright…what you saw was what you got. And everyone – from the kids to the Italian grandmothers – possessed a certain mental toughness while being kind and caring too.

Today, as a consultant, speaker and author, my world revolves around leadership and the people side of business. It was on a business trip to Philadelphia that I realized, in retrospect, that my early years were loaded with lessons – lessons I hadn't realized had permeated my adult life and altered the way I view the world. On a visit to my old neighborhood, I discovered connections between the experiences of my youth and the insights I've gained in the corporate trenches as a leader and a leaders' coach. There were valuable lessons for leaders in the streets of South Philly. Who would have thought that comic books, political corruption, schoolyard bullies, a game of Dead Box, the Ladies at the butcher shop, or a scrub brush and some Ajax would have meaning for today's leaders? Surprisingly, they do.

The same values and principles that were the foundation of my youth are the foundation of what I call StreetSavvy Leadership™. StreetSavvy Leadership is not about platitudes and theory. **It's about how to be a balanced, results-oriented leader in today's real world.** It's about dealing with the actual challenges and problems *you* face each and every day. **It's a style of leadership that you can adopt to hold people accountable and deliver results without compromising your values or being a jerk.**

StreetSavvy Leaders say what needs to be said and do what needs to be done. They are confident, candid and courageous. They are willing to acknowledge the (sometimes ugly) truth about themselves and their organizations in order to get real and get results.

What do I know about getting real and getting results? I've been where you are. I've walked the same corporate streets that you walk every day. As a leader with organizations such as Ford, GM and American Medicorp, I've experienced every challenge, problem and issue that you're facing and then some. Union-organizing campaigns, harassment cases, coaching in extremely sensitive situations, terminating friends, motivating employees during rightsizing, delivering nearly impossible results…I've been right there on the firing line. And if I haven't personally experienced it, I've coached a leader or executive who has.

The StreetSavvy Leader shares best practices of my own and from some of my most successful clients. It offers solutions that will resonate with you and work for you regardless of your background (you don't have to be from South Philly to be StreetSavvy!), your generation, level of leadership, the size of your organization, the nature of your industry, the strength of your company's bottom line or the status of the economy. And you can be confident knowing that I've used the StreetSavvy Leadership™ approach with great success in my work with some of America's most respected organizations, including GE, Wal-Mart, Neiman Marcus, ExxonMobil, Bank of America, OfficeMax, Pizza Hut, Home Depot, Securitas, the American Red Cross, the Orlando Magic, Caterpillar and Ocean Spray.

Knowing that life in the streets of Corporate America is busy and stressful, I intentionally wrote this book in a solutions-oriented, quick-read format with self-contained vignettes that even the busiest leader can read in 10 minutes or less. Each chapter stands on its own. You don't have to worry about picking up where you left off. Skip around, read what interests you, get solutions to your most pressing people-problems. And unlike other leadership books, which are about as pleasant to read as running into a group of thugs in a dark alley, *The StreetSavvy Leader* won't be boring. The 21 leadership lessons are anchored with humorous stories, unique experiences, Philly-isms and interesting characters that you'll remember long after you've finished reading.

Each chapter includes **StreetSavvy Techniques** with detailed examples, specific language and application ideas so that you can use them right now. But you will also use them comfortably and successfully over and over again – especially at 3:00 on a Thursday when you're in the middle of a crisis or dealing with employees who aren't doing their job.

Every chapter also has a section entitled **How You Doin'?** This section includes questions that will encourage you to look in the mirror, so to speak, and assess how well you are doing both individually and organizationally with respect to each leadership topic. For a big-picture perspective of how you're doin' as a StreetSavvy Leader, go to www.StreetSavvyLeader.com and take the free **StreetSavvy Leader Self-Assessment.** Keep your results as a "baseline score" against which you can measure your progress in the future.

"YROI" is another term you'll find throughout the book. It stands for *Your* Return on Investment. YROI is what *you* (not the organization) get for your investment of time, energy and resources. It's all about what's in it for you to become a better leader and how you will personally benefit from practicing StreetSavvy Leadership.

Now, I wouldn't be very StreetSavvy if I didn't give you fair warning: I believe in personal accountability. That means that I believe that **each individual is responsible for being the best leader he or she can be.** Sometimes without realizing it, leaders can cause their own problems. That's when I have no problem telling the Emperor he or she has no clothes. So be prepared to take a long, hard look in the mirror. I realize that depending on where you are in the chain of command, you may not have the authority to change the leadership culture of your organization. But you can always practice exceptional leadership and directly *influence* your team's or department's culture.

My commitment is to share with you the best advice I have based on my 35-plus years of leadership experience. My vision and my hope is that when you finish reading this book, you will be a more StreetSavvy Leader who can maneuver down any "street" and handle any situation that crosses your path.

Al Lucia
www.StreetSavvyLeader.com

How "*Youse*" Can Best *Use* This Book

Youse is another Philly-ism. UrbanDictionary.com defines it as "a South Philly term referring to several people," as in "Youse guys know where I can get a good cheesesteak?" To ensure the biggest YROI for reading this book, let me give "youse" a few suggestions:

- Read the first chapter, "Call 'Chips on the Ball'...Hold Others – and Yourself – Accountable for Results" to get a feel for the format.

- Review the Contents page and highlight the chapters that relate to your five most critical leadership challenges.

- Read each of those chapters. Highlight key points and make notes in the margins.

- Take just five minutes to do a "gut check" and answer the **How You Doin'?** questions in each chapter, jotting down notes in the space provided. These questions are designed to encourage self-reflection and develop self-awareness about your leadership beliefs, attitudes and skills. Honesty is key here.

- Study the **StreetSavvy Techniques** at the end of each chapter. Decide which ones resonate with you and are relevant for your team and circumstances. Select at least one technique and commit to putting it into action for the next 30 days. This will help ensure that the valuable ideas you find won't remain stuck in the pages of this book.

- Find a like-minded leader in your organization, professional association or networking group, and ask him/her to be your accountability partner. Accountability is one of the most crucial factors to success, and honestly, it's often difficult to have the self-discipline to hold yourself accountable for change. If you truly want to improve your leadership skills and get better results, then find someone who will encourage you, support you and hold your feet to the fire as you implement the techniques in this book.

- As you read the stories from my childhood, think back to your own childhood. I believe there are crucial lessons for each of us in our past. They are there, just waiting for us to stop, turn around and see them for what they are. What lessons did you learn growing up that can be applied to your current leadership challenges?

If you have a leadership challenge or people issue not covered in this book, feel free to contact me at AL@ADLassociates.com. Likewise, feel free to contact me if you disagree with or want to challenge any of the concepts or strategies presented here. I always welcome the opportunity to talk with other StreetSavvy Leaders!

1

Call "Chips on the Ball"... Hold Others – and Yourself – Accountable for Results

South Philadelphia in the 1950s and 1960s was a great place to be a kid.

It was a different (not necessarily simpler) time. There were no after-school programs, no video games, no organized soccer or baseball leagues. I'd walk home from school, grab a snack and head outside to play until my mother called me in for dinner…not with a cell phone, but with her voice. Dinner was on the table between 5:30 and 6:00 because that was when Dad got home from work.

During those weekday afternoons, and especially on the weekends, my friends and I played street games passed down from generations of South Philly kids. We amused ourselves for hours with games like Dead Box, Slapball, Halfball, Stickball and Hit the Penny, to name just a few. (The tradition lives on even though I no longer live in South Philly. My children know how to play Halfball and Hit the Quarter – the inflated version of Hit the Penny – and someday soon, my grandkids will too.)

We played a lot of these games with "pimple balls" – white rubber balls about the size of a tennis ball, filled with air and covered with small "pimples." We didn't have much money, so it was a big deal when one of us bought a pimple ball. Fortunately, between birthdays, holidays and Uncle Tony's cigar box, someone in the group could usually scrounge up 10 cents, and off we'd go to Ester's Candy Store on Wolf Street.

Although pimple balls were highly prized, they often got roofed (stuck on a roof) or lost during the course of a game. That meant the fun was over for everyone. And that's precisely why, within seconds of plunking down his two nickels for a pimple ball, the new owner would call out for all to hear, "Chips on the ball!"

In South Philly lingo, "chips on the ball" meant *You lose it, you pay for it!* So, if I called "chips" on a new pimple ball, and during a fierce game of stickball Joe smacked it onto a roof or sent it careening down the gutter, he was on the hook to either buy a new one or pay me back. It was pure street accountability. Even as kids, we took personal responsibility for our actions.

Now don't get me wrong. When a ball was lost, there was plenty of discussion about who was at fault – Joe for hitting the ball too hard or Danny for not catching it. But in the end, whether it was an accident or a missed play, the group would have made certain Joe lived up to his commitment to get another ball. He absolutely didn't like it, but we held him accountable nonetheless.

We didn't think much about accountability back then. People simply did what they needed to do. Today, many people do the same and live up to their commitments. But there are more and more people who either never learned personal accountability or view it as unimportant. As a society, we too often let people off the hook and excuse them from living up to their responsibilities and society's standards. It happens in our legal system, in our schools and most definitely in our businesses. I wish I had a buck for every time a leader has asked me, "How can I get my people to do their job?" In my opinion, **lack of accountability is one of the top (if not *the* top) leadership problems in business today.**

What exactly does *accountability* mean? The etymology, or origins, of the word date back to Ancient Greece. When a person borrowed money from a merchant he was then held responsible *to their account*. Hence, the standard dictionary definition is: "the state of being called to account; liable; answerable." I like WordReference.com's definition: "responsibility to someone or for some activity." But the meaning of the word has evolved over time. A more common notion today is that accountability is less something one is held to and instead reflects personal choice and willingness to contribute to an outcome. Maybe that's part of the problem.

This contemporary definition is indicative of what I see in many organizations today: people getting by, just doing the minimum, going by the letter of the job rather than the spirit of it. For example: a painter paints a wall but paints over the outlets and switches in the process; an analyst crunches the numbers, but doesn't consider whether they are the right numbers or whether the information is relevant; a cashier acts as if she can't believe a customer had the nerve to interrupt her with a question.

Did the people in these examples do their jobs? Technically, I suppose they did. The painter painted, the analyst analyzed, and the cashier "checked out" (maybe in both senses of the phrase). But I think we can all agree that none of these people fulfilled the spirit of their jobs.

Call me idealistic, but to me it's pretty simple: accountability is doing the job you were hired to do and doing it to the best of your ability. You either do the job or you don't. Back in Philly, calling "chips on the ball" was in effect an agreement that everyone would live up to their responsibilities and uphold their end of the bargain. In a business sense, calling "chips on the ball" is the agreement made between an individual and an organization, where both parties agree to live up to their commitments and do their part. The organization agrees to pay the individual for successfully completing certain duties and tasks, and the individual agrees to perform those duties and tasks *successfully and completely*, day in and day out.

Consider for a moment an interview situation: You're interviewing a candidate for a job and the session is going well. At the end of the interview, you ask, "If we hire you, will you do this job?" If the candidate were to say, "Well, I'm not sure" or "Sometimes, but not every day," would you hire that person? I hope not. And yet in reality we tolerate those same "responses" on a daily basis from people who already work for us.

So here's the $64,000 question: If 10-year-old kids playing games can hold each other accountable for results, why can't we? Why are leaders oftentimes hesitant or even embarrassed to ask people to do their jobs? I think there are three interrelated reasons why we don't do a better job of holding ourselves and others accountable:

1. Unclear, inconsistent and unrealistic expectations.

> A sales manager once lamented to me that his salespeople weren't "connecting enough with prospects and customers." In his mind, they were goofing off, as evidenced by the fact that they routinely left early. I asked him, "What does 'connect enough' mean?"
>
> He said, "You know…enough to keep the pipeline full."
>
> Then I asked, "Well, how full is full enough? How many prospects do you want in the pipeline? How many cold calls and follow-up calls are salespeople required to make each day?"

He just stared at me. He couldn't give me an answer.

You can't hold people accountable to a vague concept or moving target. It would be like calling just "Chips!" Chips on what? The ball? The comic book? The toy? If you don't set, communicate and stick to absolutely crystal-clear terms about what, how, when, where and even why employees are to do their jobs, you're dead in the water.

We live in an instant-gratification culture. We need it, want it, have to have it *now,* and that sets up unrealistic expectations about what can be done and when. Don't set objectives for yourself or your team that you know from the start can't be met or aren't workable because of competing priorities.

Set clear, consistent, realistic expectations. What exactly are the duties and responsibilities of the job? What specifically are the standards to which the job should be done? Precisely when should the project be completed? Who does one answer to?

2. Doing "the job" has become optional because there are no true consequences for *not* doing it.

Let's assume for a moment that one of the requirements of your job is to complete a monthly production report by the 10th day of the following month. Last month you didn't get the report done on time. You had a good reason: a key employee was out on leave, and you had to cover his job as well as your own. But the truth is that you didn't hold yourself accountable. When you finally deliver the report to your manager on the 12th, she doesn't say a word about it being late. In fact, she doesn't even look at it for another three days. She didn't take responsibility for holding you accountable either.

What do you think you'll do this month? Will you feel the same urgency and responsibility to get the report done on time? Will anything happen if you let it slide another day or two?

When there are no meaningful consequences for not producing agreed-upon results, eventually standards and requirements lose their meaning and their power. They become arbitrary, even optional. When employees can get away with not helping the customer or doing a poor job on the project, they rightfully conclude that the customer or project isn't that important. (After all, if it were, they would have to answer to someone for why it wasn't done.) As a result, **lack of accountability isn't just tolerated, it's actually "rewarded."** Over time, not holding people accountable for results becomes part of the corporate culture. Obviously it's not overtly stated, but it's part of the culture nonetheless.

Too many leaders don't have the courage to look their employees in the eye and say, "Do your job." Why? Because too often they feel they don't have any real options if employees don't do their jobs.

In my father's day, if an employee didn't do his job, he was fired…quickly! When my brother and I were kids, if our mother or father told us to be quiet or go to our rooms, we did it. It never entered our minds not to comply. It simply wasn't an option. But society has changed – with respect to both employment and child rearing. Changes in employment laws were absolutely needed, appropriate and valuable. But perhaps the pendulum has swung so far to the other side that leaders today don't feel they have any choice but to allow poor performance to continue.

If you take steps to hold employees accountable for results, will senior leadership back you up? If an employee fails to produce results and you terminate him or her, will it hold up with the union, with the EEOC, or in court if the company is sued? If you terminate an employee and you can't find a qualified replacement right away, or if a hiring freeze is in effect and you can't get a replacement at all, who's left holding the bag? You! These are the questions that make us pause and wonder if perhaps a warm body doing some of the job is better than no body at all.

3. Participatory management blurs the lines of accountability.

Back in the days of authoritarian management, employees were told to "tote the barge," so to speak. And they did it, no questions asked. When the lines of authority are clear, it isn't terribly complicated to hold people to their responsibilities.

But with the rise and popularity of concepts such as participatory management, employee involvement and Six Sigma, the issue of accountability becomes far more complex. It's no longer a matter of simply "toting the barge." Employees want a voice in how they tote the barge, when they will tote the barge, who else should help tote the barge and how big the barge should be. Oh, and they want to know why they are toting barges in the first place!

Participatory management increases employee engagement and typically provides better outcomes as well. At the same time, it makes holding people accountable far more challenging. That's just the price you pay. Is it more complicated? Yes. Is it doable? Definitely! (More on exactly how to hold people accountable in the **StreetSavvy Techniques** section at the end of the chapter.)

For the most part, the accountability problem in business today isn't due to a lack of caring. The leaders I know care a great deal. It is true they need some real-world solutions for *how* to hold employees accountable for doing their jobs in a litigation-happy, ever-more-complex environment. But the real issue is that they've come to believe that accountability and responsibility aren't all that important because *their* leaders don't hold *them* accountable.

Accountability is a two-sided issue, up and down the entire chain of command. On the one side, too many individuals don't practice personal accountability, whether intentionally or unknowingly. On the other side, too many leaders don't hold their employees accountable. Please understand, I'm not singling you out. Most of the leaders I work with are facing the same issue. You're not alone. We've all done it. And you know what? It's hard to hold people accountable. But that doesn't mean we shouldn't do it.

As a leader, practice personal accountability *and* hold your team members accountable for results, whether anyone else in the organization does or not. Why? It's simple…what would happen if every person on your team consistently did his or her job? Would *your* job be easier? Would you be less stressed? Would your spouse and kids like being around you again? Absolutely! Now that's what I call a high YROI!

So really, it's not an issue of *if* you should hold people accountable, it's *how* you do it. In my experience, many leaders mistakenly believe that the way to hold employees accountable for results is through fear, intimidation and, if necessary, punishment. (No wonder many are hesitant to practice accountability!) Fear does work, but it works counter to what this book is all about – smart leadership. Intimidation and punishment are compliance-based methods of accountability that may produce short-term results. Unfortunately, they also irreparably damage trust, commitment and engagement. Insulting or humiliating employees, giving them demeaning assignments, suspending them without pay, and threatening them with termination will definitely get a reaction…just not the kind of reaction you want!

Hold Others – and Yourself – Accountable for Results

Holding people accountable for doing their jobs doesn't have to be a harsh, unpleasant experience – for them or you. For more than 25 years, I've been coaching leaders on how to effectively use a non-punitive approach to accountability. This simple yet validated approach is based on the concept that effective accountability occurs when people are respected, treated as adults, and coached instead of punished for accountability gaps. (See the **StreetSavvy Techniques** at the end of the chapter for more on this approach.)

There are plenty of organizations out there who are doing accountability right. The Container Store is a great example. Since its founding in 1978, superior customer service has been a core goal and value of this award-winning retailer. One of the secrets to the company's success is that it holds its customer-service people accountable for the *way* they provide service.

One of my larger clients, an international equipment manufacturer, also stands out when it comes to accountability. Employee engagement is a key piece of their 20-year vision. To ensure that engagement happens, every level of the organization is held accountable. Engagement is measured through annual, worldwide employee-opinion surveys. Executives routinely discuss engagement issues, and leaders' engagement results are a factor in performance appraisals, merit increases, bonuses and succession-planning decisions.

Most of the people on your team are more than willing to be held accountable *if* your expectations are clear, consistent and reasonable, and you treat them with respect. They truly want to know when they have performance or accountability issues, and they want your help in fixing them. So I encourage you to usher in a new day (in an old way.) In fact, I dare you to walk into your next team meeting and say, "Chips on the ball! Let's talk about accountability."

How *You* Doin'?

➢ Do you hold yourself accountable for results and for the commitments you make to others?

➢ Do you hold the people on your team accountable and thereby model this behavior for the rest of the organization?

➢ Is it possible that you foster a lack of accountability through inadequate performance-review preparation or insufficient coaching?

➢ When was the last time you checked with your internal customers to find out if they think your department is accountable for its responsibilities?

StreetSavvy Techniques

The key to holding people accountable is in the method. So let's put this non-punitive approach to accountability into action:

Step 1: **Establish crystal-clear, reasonable responsibilities and expectations that people can be held to.** It's neither appropriate nor fair to hold people accountable for generalities such as "Do a good job," "Provide *WOW* customer service," or "Deliver contracting excellence." How is a team member to know if she has effectively accomplished such a vague task? Perhaps her definition of "excellence" is different than yours.

Numbers, specific timeframes and measurable results provide better direction and allow for true accountability. For example: "Complete the entire report, including the financial analysis, by March 16th," is a definitive statement against which employees can be held accountable. Either they achieve the result or they don't.

Step 2: **Build a relationship through day-to-day recognition and coaching.** These two activities create the maximum impact in developing accountability and therefore should represent the bulk of the interactions you have with your employees. Recognition and coaching together send the message that accountability is a priority.

First, consistently recognize those who follow through on their commitments and meet or exceed the expectations you set out in Step 1. What gets recognized and reinforced gets repeated.

Second, when there are gaps between expected and actual results or behavior, positively coach employees for continuous performance-improvement. There are two essential elements of this process:

1. Clearly describe the impact of the individual's behavior and lack of accountability, especially with respect to the team, the organization and business results.

2. Carefully explain the specific, logical consequences that will occur if the individual doesn't correct the problem.

For example, Sean is a maintenance person on A-shift. Sean hasn't been completing all of his job duties, primarily, repairing and maintaining production equipment. You've determined that Sean's responsibilities are reasonable – the individuals with the same job on B and C shifts are able to consistently accomplish the assignments – and Sean has told you that he clearly understands his duties.

In a coaching session with him, you might say something like, "Sean, when you don't finish your repairs, the next shift has to not only complete your work, but also finish their own. In addition, having equipment down for repairs for more than one shift slows down the entire line, making it difficult for your co-workers to meet their production quotas. As you might imagine, that causes them to be frustrated and feel animosity toward you. And finally, your lack of accountability costs the organization money because the line is not working efficiently, and that directly affects your bonus as well as everyone else's." (For more details on coaching, see Chapter 16.)

Step 3: **Take action to address ongoing accountability gaps.** If, after coaching, an employee continues to demonstrate a lack of accountability, move to more serious interventions such as formal discipline. Remember that discipline and punishment are two different things. You don't have to scare, intimidate or threaten people into accountability, but you do need to be firm. If you've built a solid relationship with employees and earned their trust, they will feel you have their best interests at heart, even in serious situations.

Step 4: **Follow up.** Take appropriate action based on the employee's response to coaching or formal discipline. If he adequately addresses his accountability issues, extend congratulations. If, however, the employee doesn't make a positive correction, expand his employment opportunities…outside of your organization. Have the courage to terminate those who refuse to be accountable for their commitments and job responsibilities. This will quickly send the message that you and your organization are serious about accountability.

2

"Look! It's a Bird! It's a Plane! It's Superman!"... Discover the Superhuman Power of Comic Book Communication

Some of the best moments of my childhood revolved around comic books. I'd labor long and hard to save enough money until, finally, the day would come when I had ten cents. Then I'd walk down to the candy store or Schwartz's Drugstore and spend 30 minutes trying to decide which one to buy. Superman? Batman? Captain Marvel? It was a thrilling dilemma for a 10-year-old kid. (By the way, do you know how old these superheroes are? They first appeared in 1938, 1939 and 1940, respectively!)

Most trips to the store for pimple balls, baseball cards or candy were made in the company of friends or my brother, Rich. But buying a comic book was different. I always tried to go alone. Once I'd made my purchase, I'd find a quiet place, usually my bedroom, where I'd spend hours absorbing every picture and word. It was a great escape from parents, school and the world in general.

I usually read a new comic book at least three times before showing my prized possession to a friend and running the risk of it getting messed up. We traded comics within our group of friends, but there was nothing better than the fresh, crisp pages of a brand new comic book. The characters, the stories, the colors

– they were mesmerizing. Could Superman defeat his nemesis, Lex Luthor? Would the citizens of Gotham City discover the Dark Knight's true identity? What did the evil mad scientist Doctor Sivana have in store this time for The World's Mightiest Mortal? I hung on every word and couldn't wait for the next new comic book to come out.

Wouldn't it be great if employees felt the same way about our written communications?

When I look at how communication is handled in Corporate America, I find absolutely no parallels with comic book magic. Employees **are not** anxiously anticipating your next memo, they trashed the five pages of policy changes, and they have anything but enthusiasm for yet anther broadcast email. And when it comes to employees reading these communications – and identifying and remembering the relevant information – you can *fugettaboutit!*

Perhaps you think that business communications and comic books *shouldn't* have anything in common and that the way to inform and appeal to adults is completely different than with kids. If so, perhaps that's the problem!

Now, you might wonder where I get off implying you have a problem communicating effectively. Don't take it personally. I don't know if you and your organization have communication challenges or not, but I know there are many that do. Despite valid efforts to improve communication, research and surveys indicate it's still one of the biggest problems organizations face. In fact, recent studies by Deloitte and Hay Group revealed that, in a time when they need to know more clearly than ever what to do and why, employees are experiencing "information fatigue."

We're living in a time when face-to-face and even verbal communication is taking a distant back seat to new written forms of communication. Memos are on their way out, replaced by intranet postings, abbreviated emails, text messaging and even tweets. As communication becomes more impersonal and condensed, there's more room for inaccuracy and omissions, and a greater chance that essential information won't receive the attention and focus it deserves. According to the U.K. Institute of Management and Aspen Briskness Communications, despite the increased use of email and computers, 55 percent of employees say the relevance of information reaching them has grown worse or not changed.

Further complicating the issue is that leaders are often the middlemen and middlewomen in business communications. Think about it…how often do you receive communication from senior leadership, human resources or other departments about the state of the organization, policy or procedural changes, organizational structure changes, benefits, financial results, competitive information, new positions, inventory reports, customer service results and issues, production and output reports, etc.? And don't forget all the department- or team-specific information that originates from or must be shared within your group: project-related specifics, meeting schedules and agendas, roles and responsibilities, productivity results, detailed work instructions, and so on.

Holy Moley! It's enough to make you want to retreat to the Batcave and forget about communicating with the outside world.

But that's not an option for today's leaders. In the Information Age and beyond, effective communication isn't about quantity or even quality. **Successful communication means your messages to employees are received, understood, internalized and, if necessary, applied.**

Communication is at the heart of any relationship, professional or personal. And ineffective communication is the root cause of many unnecessary challenges, from union organizing attempts to marital strife. Just as Kryptonite nullifies Superman's powers, immobilizes him and will eventually kill him, poor communication nullifies trust and respect, immobilizes productivity and eventually will negatively affect results. For example, unclear instructions regarding maintenance of a clean room in a microelectronics facility can lead to poor quality and defective products. In an industry such as healthcare, inaccurate communication can truly have life and death consequences.

A critical part of your job as a leader is to dig through the onslaught of information, determine what is important to your team and then communicate that information to your employees in a meaningful way. You must step up and become the champion of powerful communication for your employees. In fact… perhaps your superhero alter ego is none other than…**Captain Communication**! Yes! You are faster than a speeding bullet, more powerful than a locomotive, and able to leap tall stacks of copious memos and unnecessary emails in a single bound! You must battle information overload and defeat employee disinterest. You must use your leadership powers to shine the light on critical information that relates to and affects employees' jobs and responsibilities.

Am I serious? Absolutely! Perhaps if we as leaders would lighten up about communication, our employees might take it more seriously.

There's a lot we can learn about effective communication from the comic book genre. Consider the following: In comic books, a lot happens in just a few pages. There is equal emphasis on words and pictures. The goal is to hold the reader's attention and interest. Color and design are used to engage the reader. The cover sells you on the story, and the story is easy to remember and share with others. The most important scenes are highlighted with bigger boxes or captions, or even an entire page. And finally, comic books are *entertaining!*

One of my client organizations, a well-respected national retailer, truly understands the importance of communication and the value of creative, individualized messages. This forward-thinking company supports its leaders by providing them with summaries of complex issues and the time needed for one-on-one meetings with employees to address critical issues. They hold leaders accountable for effective communication and formally evaluate and recognize efforts in this area through their performance appraisal system.

One store manager who placed a top priority on accurate, meaningful communication was eventually promoted to lead corporate training as a direct result of his innovative communication methods. Another supervisor, preparing for a team meeting to explain a written policy change, asked her team members to suggest songs that related to the issue being communicated. As people gathered for the meeting, she played "We Can Work It Out" on a boom box. Do you think they remembered the key points of the policy change and how it affected their jobs? You bet! Clearly, this was an approach that wouldn't have worked with the typical email blast or "all-employee" notice on the bulletin board.

Actually, when it comes to effective communication, there is no such thing as "for all employees." If you want employees to read, retain and apply information, you have to individualize the message. Perhaps you're thinking you don't have time to give that kind of attention to your communication. Just remember that studies show the more general and broad-based the communication, the less effective it is.

So why should you invest the time to make your communications more creative and individualized? What's the YROI?

> **Gain understanding, support and acceptance**. General, non-specific communication geared to the masses leads to non-compliance and inaction. On the other hand, individualized communication that clearly identifies why the information is relevant to employees, their jobs and their lives leads to understanding, support and acceptance of the message and ultimately to action. Which would you rather have from your team?

> **Enhance productivity**. With accurate work instructions and policies and procedures, there's a much better chance that people will handle their responsibilities correctly and quickly. Crystal clear communication ultimately saves more time than it takes to create because employees don't have to keep coming back to you with questions, issues and concerns.

Several years ago, there was a popular TV show called *The Wonder Years*. That phrase describes how I feel about my youth, and one of my fondest memories of those wonder years was reading comic books. I liked other books too, but the comics – stories presented in a way kids could relate to – really engaged me. Maybe that's the ultimate solution to effective communication: **ask employees what type of communication engages them**. I'd love to see one of them pull out a comic book and show it to you in response. *Shazam!* Wouldn't that be cool?!

How *You* Doin'?

- Do your team members frequently say, "This is the first I've heard about it" or "I never received that memo/email" even though you know the information was sent?

- Do you spill out more words than people have time – or care – to read?

- Are your communication pieces fresh and innovative, or is every communication the same as the one before in terms of layout, style, emphasis, authorship, etc.?

- In your communications, do you highlight the benefits to employees and the impact of the information on their jobs?

StreetSavvy Techniques

Put some *"Bang!"* and *"Zowie!"* in your communications. If you ratchet it up just a bit, you'll be a better communicator than most leaders in America.

1. Develop a keen awareness for the fact that people receive information differently even though most leaders use the same communication piece for everyone. Are your employees mostly right-brain creative people or left-brain numbers people? What is their education level? Which generation do they belong to? What kind of personalities do they have? What is each team member's dominant learning style – visual, auditory or kinesthetic?

Repackage essential communication to meet receivers' needs. If the original language is complex or filled with jargon, rewrite it in a more reader-friendly format. Since most people are visual learners, use pictures, graphics, charts, graphs and other visuals whenever possible.

2. Communicate only the essential elements of each message and offer to provide more information for those who are interested in the details. Information dumps do very little to provide knowledge. Identify the critical pieces of information that employees need to do their jobs and ensure those key issues are highlighted. For example, from a two-page memo, determine which three issues have the most impact on your team and list those in bullet form near the beginning of your repackaged communication.

3. Think "2.8-second gut grabber." You only have a few seconds to capture people's attention and draw them into your communication piece, so **openings are critical.** Become a master storyteller instead of a rote reporter. As you create each piece, think about how the cover of a comic book grabs the reader's attention and sets up the story...Lois Lane perilously dangles from a building; Superman withers away as Kryptonite hangs over his head; Batman, tied to a bomb, desperately struggles to free himself.

Work to emulate that technique in your pieces. Create interest or suspense from the get-go. Make certain your subject line points out how employees will be affected or what's in it for them to continue reading or to click on the link. (Remember that a link to a posting on your intranet is even easier to ignore than a piece of paper in an inbox!)

For example, instead of a subject line that reads, "ABC Company Signs Contract with New Client," try something like, "ABC Company Gets Revenue Boost." If you're sharing the results of your customer survey, you could use a headline such as "What Our Customers Are Saying About *You*!" For an announcement about a new vacation policy, try opening with, "What does the new vacation policy mean for you?" For reporting financial results: "Did quarterly earnings exceed projections or fall short? What does it mean for *your* bonus?"

Consider opening a meeting with a story or appropriate joke rather than simply making an announcement. Instead of a boring email about signing up for security training, tell a brief fictional story about an employee who missed training and found herself in a jam. If your communication pieces are interesting (or dare I say, entertaining), you will dramatically increase the chances that they'll be read. Who knows, you might even reach a point when employees eagerly await your next communiqué!

3

Say "Hunks!"... Use Unwritten Rules to Get More of What You Want

"HUNKS!"

No, I'm not talking about the way some women refer to handsome men.

"Hunks" is a term my friends and I used growing up to stake a claim to someone else's candy. It's similar to calling

A typical candy store in South Philly. Don't forget to say, "Hunks!!"

"Shotgun!" to proclaim your right to sit in the front passenger seat of the car. So if I had a Hershey bar or TastyKake and a friend said, "Hunks!" before I could say, "No hunks!" I was compelled by an unwritten rule of the streets to give him a piece. And when you're a kid who doesn't get to buy candy very often, the last thing you want to do is share it! But there was no hesitation. If we didn't abide by the Hunks Rule, we knew we'd have to face the consequences. On the other hand, it was great if someone else was buying the candy, and you were fast enough to yell, "Hunks!"

I'd forgotten about the Hunks Rule until years later when my brother, Rich, came to town for a visit. We were eating at a local restaurant, and as the waiter set a piece of decadent chocolate cake in front of me, Rich emphatically said, "Hunks!" When I finally stopped laughing, I gave him a bite.

We got to talking about how powerful that implicit rule was for us as kids and how Hunks wasn't the only unwritten rule of the streets. Chips on the Ball was another important one, as was the rule that the boy *always* paid for the girl on a date. Likewise, everyone knew that the best athletes would be the team captains when it came time to pick teams for street games. There was an unspoken rule that you never said anything nice about a teacher for fear of being labeled a brownnoser or teacher's pet. And then there was the very annoying Birthday Punch Rule where, on your birthday, your friends punched you in the arm once for every year plus an extra punch for good luck (that one was always the hardest). Ah…good times.

Not long after that dinner, I was working with a client organization when one of its leaders confided in me, "No one around here reports bad news 'up the line' because the messenger always gets shot." It occurred to me then that, just like in the streets of my youth, there are plenty of unwritten rules in organizations, and they are, indeed, quite powerful.

Unfortunately, it seems that many unwritten rules are counterproductive to organizational success. Do you recognize any of the following unwritten rules within your organization?

- ➢ Use your entire budget every year because if you don't, next year management will cut your budget and allocate it to someone else.
- ➢ Always ask for more resources than you need to accomplish an assignment or project.

- If you compliment your boss or senior leadership, you'll be labeled "a company man/woman"...or something worse.
- Do only the bare minimum. Doing your work faster or better only gets you more work. And in the long run, it doesn't matter how hard you work anyway because the performance appraisal system results in meaningless, if any, raises.
- If you can't finish your work during the work week, you'd better be in the office over the weekend.
- "Face time" gets you promoted.

Stop for just a moment and consider the real-world, down-stream impact of these rules on a leader, an organization, its culture, its customers, its finances and, ultimately, its shareholders.

If you're like me, you probably have a pit in your stomach.

Fortunately, not all unwritten rules are negative. Some create positive effects:

- Everyone pitches in to get a project completed on time.
- We cover for each other when one of us has a "life" situation.
- If you want to move up in the organization, you have to be a good people person and build successful relationships.
- If we don't see you at the monthly departmental lunch or Friday-afternoon gathering, we'll come drag you out of your cubicle or office and make you have some fun with us.

Negative or positive, detrimental or beneficial, there's no getting around it – **unwritten rules form the framework of your organization's true culture.** Author Steve Simpson says, "Unwritten rules are people's perceptions of 'the way we do things around here.' They are most prominent in casual discussions between staff, in the talk that occurs after meetings, and in the difference between what people say and what people do."

So who "writes" these unwritten rules?

I bet you're thinking, "Employees." Nope! Unwritten rules are usually created by leaders, although they often don't realize they're doing it. Unwritten rules are the result of signals sent by management: who gets promoted (and who gets passed over), who gets the good projects, how people are treated, how information is communicated, what gets attention, what gets recognized, what are the priorities, etc. Employees carefully observe leaders' attitudes and actions – like which behaviors are rewarded and which are "punished" – and learn to act accordingly. And because these guidelines are founded on employees' personal experiences, they tend to have far more emotional impact, and therefore a greater effect on behavior, than official policies and procedures.

Did you notice in the previous lists of unwritten rules that the negative ones have more emotional "oomph" than the positive ones? This means they also have a more significant impact on the organization's culture.

Because unwritten rules are obviously not part of the policies and procedures manual, many leaders think of them as "soft stuff." As a result, they are often either flat-out ignored or, at a minimum, get little attention. But the power and influence of unwritten rules are real, whether you're aware of their existence or not. Be forewarned that a lack of awareness minimizes your effectiveness as a leader. If you assume that your team members are only operating under the written rules, then you are missing a big piece of what is truly going on day to day, what is driving people's behaviors and actions, and why employees are less productive than they could be.

Use Unwritten Rules to Get More of What You Want

Just in case you doubt the power of unwritten rules, let me tell you a story: A restaurant manager had heard a rumor that it was usual practice for his employees to give new hires a bit of a hard time. The truth is, the actions were borderline harassment, but the manager did nothing about the unwritten rule. Eventually, a new busboy didn't think the team's little "initiation" was too funny and quit. When the busboy sued the company for constructive discharge, senior leadership didn't think it was funny either, and the manager was fired.

While negative unwritten rules can be harmful to your career if ignored, positive unwritten rules can increase your influence as a leader and be your ally in enhancing employee accountability. I have a couple of clients who have a fantastic unwritten rule: employees hold each other accountable. Officially of course, these employees have no authority over one another and can't force co-workers to behave in certain ways. So where does this peer accountability come from if it's not a company policy? Peer pressure creates "friendly persuasion." It's fascinating how a constructive comment from a peer can be logically and rationally accepted, whereas that same comment from someone in leadership can elicit a very different and defensive reaction.

The leaders in these organizations make a *conscious* effort to nurture and support this unwritten peer accountability rule. They've figured out that the more committed and engaged employees are, the less they need to use compliance-type approaches to accountability. The influence of this implied principle throughout these organizations is very real and so are the results.

Many leaders fear they will lose control of employees if they encourage behaviors and actions that aren't "by the book." These leaders fail to understand that unwritten rules exist anyway. Seems to me you might as well use them to your benefit.

Many aspects of growing up on the streets of South Philly left a major impression on me. But honestly, the concept of unwritten rules never struck me as one of those life-influencing kind of things. Who would have thought that sharing one piece of candy with a friend who said, "Hunks" would lead to an appreciation of the tremendous power and influence of unwritten rules in business?

By the way, let me take care of something right now. If I ever run into you in a restaurant or candy store…No hunks!

And you can write that down!

How *You* Doin'?

- What unwritten rules are at work in your organization?

- How often do you ask employees about their perceptions regarding rules, both written and unwritten? Are your team members comfortable enough with you to share the truth about your organization's unwritten rules?

- Do you help keep negative unwritten rules alive by either ignoring their existence or unconsciously reinforcing them?

- Do you reinforce the behaviors that result from positive unwritten rules, such as employees voluntarily covering shifts for others who are having life challenges?

StreetSavvy Techniques

How can you minimize the effects of negative unwritten rules and enhance and operationalize the positive ones?

1. Identify the unwritten rules in your organization. Spend some time carefully observing work flow. Listen closely to the complaints of employees and other leaders at all levels. Talk to people who are leaving the organization. You'll soon see patterns emerge. Some pointed questions to carefully selected individuals such as, "Is this the way things really work around here...?" will confirm your suspicions regarding unwritten rules.

If you have difficulty identifying positive unwritten rules in your organization, don't worry. You're not alone. But there is a solution: start some yourself. My friend Bud created an unwritten rule in his company in which employees are encouraged to find opportunities to recognize clients for professional or personal accomplishments. Bud then gives the nominated client a small token of congratulations. A formal policy has never been instituted, but over the last ten years, hundreds of clients have received recognition from Bud and his employees.

2. Publicly acknowledge the existence of your unwritten rules and get them in sync with your formal rules. Determine if any of your positive unwritten rules conflict with stated policies and procedures. Often times organizations actually operate under a set of unwritten rules that contradict outdated procedures still technically in effect, but no one takes the time to make appropriate updates. You'd be surprised how often this happens. Perhaps your policy manual outlines a punitive-based discipline system, but leaders don't follow it because your organizational values and culture emphasize treating employees as adults and with respect. Or maybe you have a rule on the books that states every employee must work a double shift every two months. However, it hasn't been followed in years, and there's been no detrimental effect on productivity.

It's important that your written and unwritten rules be in sync. You don't want to inadvertently kill the very influences that are likely a large part of your success.

3. **Minimize the impact of negative rules and harness the power of positive ones to shape your culture.** For example, consider your unwritten rules when selecting new employees or promoting existing team members. If you find evidence that a candidate encourages and practices destructive rules, ask yourself if you want that person on your team or in a leadership role. Conversely, candidates who exemplify the beneficial tenets of your organization will further help weave those behaviors into the fabric of your culture.

Recognize and reinforce behaviors that perpetuate positive unwritten rules, especially those that involve customers (internal and external). Take every opportunity in meetings and internal communications to publicize employees who demonstrate the specific behaviors that are written nowhere but reflect on the positive aspects of your organization's culture. This is just one more example of the "bang for the buck" you get from providing recognition.

4

Stop the Broad Street Bullies... Start with Yourself

When they hear the name "Philadelphia," many people think of a rough city full of gangsters, thugs and bullies. This notion was so prevalent in the past that the nickname for Philly's National Hockey League team, the Flyers, was for many years "The Broad Street Bullies." They were well known throughout the league for fighting and playing dirty.

Now you might think I'd disagree with this less-than-flattering characterization of my hometown and try to paint a different picture. Not so. In fact, I think we definitely had more than our share of bullies in South Philly. The Italian immigrants who settled in many South Philly neighborhoods were often relegated to physically demanding, rough jobs at the docks or in factories. They learned quickly to defend themselves, and it was natural for them to teach their children to stand up for themselves and not let others push them around. Some of these kids took that lesson to the next level, becoming overly aggressive and confrontational. They lived by the creed that it was better to mess with someone than to let someone mess with you.

No kid likes to deal with bullies, and I was no different. I never got beat up, just hit a few times and pushed around a lot. The physical pain bullies inflicted was usually overshadowed by the pain of embarrassment and humiliation they imposed. Being teased about playing the violin in front of the entire grade or being forced to give up your lunch money created a feeling that went way past your empty stomach and found its way to your self-esteem. Their intimidation was more mental and emotional than physical. In fact, they didn't even have to touch you, or threaten to touch you, to instill fear. The bullies knew this, too, and it actually fed their egos in some sick way.

In South Philly, the bullies hung together in groups. Their favorite tactic was the "he said you said…" Catch-22. One would approach you and say something like, "Joe here tells me that you said I'm a jerk." If you denied it, you were in essence calling Joe a liar. That would get you beat up. If you lied and acknowledged saying it, you got beat up anyway. You learned quickly that if they started to pull that trick on you, either you ran or you took your best shot and then ran! Actually, I took a more proactive approach: if I saw a group of bullies coming toward me, I did whatever I had to do to avoid them, even if it meant walking three blocks out of my way.

I thought I'd dealt with my last bully the day I walked out of the schoolyard. Years later, I realized some of them had followed me into adulthood. You can find adult bullies just about anywhere – on the freeway, at sporting events, in the parents' association, and yes, in the workplace. Workplace bullies are nothing but bad news for people, organizations and even results.

According to the Workplace Bullying Institute, workplace bullying is "the repeated, health-harming mistreatment of one or more persons (the targets) by one or more perpetrators that takes one or more of the following forms:

- ➢ verbal abuse;

- threatening, humiliating or offensive behavior/actions;
- work interference – sabotage – which prevents work from getting done."

You may be surprised to learn that workplace bullying is not always a top-down phenomenon. Although some bullies are leaders, they can also be peers and even subordinates. However, it's not hard to figure out that bullies in leadership roles are the most damaging to both people and organizational results. Here are a few other interesting facts about bullies (from the Workplace Bullying Institute Report on Abusive Workplaces):

- Woman-on-woman bullying represents 50 percent of all workplace bullying; man-on-woman bullying represents 30 percent.
- Targets are predominantly college-educated, veteran employees in their forties who had experience with their employer before being targeted.
- Average duration of bullying is 23 months.
- Bullies are likely to torment more than a single target in the work unit.
- In only 25 percent of cases is the target a member of a "protected status" group and the bully is not. In 15 percent of cases, the bully is the one who is "protected."
- Once targeted, bullied individuals face a 70 percent chance of losing their jobs.
- Perpetrators face a low risk of being held accountable: only 9 percent of bullies are transferred or terminated.

Experts agree that the potential effects of bullying on employees include anxiety, depression, damage to self-esteem and medical issues such as gastrointestinal disorders, high blood pressure and substance abuse. The human toll is without question the most critical issue, but it's also important to recognize that bullying takes a toll on the organization. Companies with bullies in strategic positions operate in compliance mode rather than commitment mode. As a result, disengagement, absenteeism and turnover are rampant.

Workplace bullying isn't new. It's been going on as long as there have been employers and employees, bosses and workers. In the days of the Industrial Revolution, a compliance-based culture worked for organizations. With an abundance of laborers, high turnover wasn't an issue. If a line worker quit because his boss was harassing him to turn out more widgets faster, there were people lined up to take his spot.

But in today's service economy, bullying has a much greater negative impact. Work gets done, but the fear created in compliance-based environments produces short-term results at best. Over time, organizations will pay the price. Bullied employees are rarely in the right frame of mind to provide basic let alone exceptional customer service. In the end, it's the customer who must deal with the byproducts of this dysfunctional approach to employee relations, and that can't be good for the bottom line.

Bullies operate in the work environment a bit more subtly than schoolyard bullies. Although some do use or threaten violence, most use their position and title rather than their fists to intimidate others. Like schoolyard bullies, their impact is more mental and emotional than physical. They seemingly exist not only to be served, but also to put others down in the process. In fact, they are the antithesis of servant leaders. These bullies act as if there is a definite caste system and they are on top. Belittling, ignoring and talking down to people are their preferred communication methods. Taking credit for work others have created and showing people up are just a few more ways bullies move through business life.

Although some workplace bullies are fully aware of their personas, I'm convinced many are either clueless or in denial. These leaders justify their actions by describing their leadership style as "in charge/in control," "focused," "direct," "no nonsense" and even "honest."

We could probably debate for hours the factors that cause someone to be a workplace bully. But in the end, it doesn't really matter, because we have no control over the cause. The best we can do is work to change the behaviors and the consequences. Which brings us to the question, why are workplace bullies allowed to continue their ways in an otherwise enlightened twenty-first century, in organizations that clearly state their interest in and respect for employees?

First, just like the kid who had his/her lunch money taken by the bully at school and was too ashamed or afraid to tell anyone, bullied employees (and even those who witness bullying) are often too embarrassed or intimidated to report the harassment. A just-released survey by the American Management Association reports that 21 percent of workers have personally observed abusive or intimidating behaviors towards employees. But I suspect there is far more bullying going on than is being reported. In fact, the Workplace Bullying Institute reports that 40 percent of targets never tell their employers and that bullying is often erroneously branded as "conflict" or a "difference in personality styles." As a result, those who are in a position to do something about bullying often aren't aware of the problem or its magnitude. And you can't fix a problem you don't know exists.

Second, all too often, employees who do have the guts to report bullying frequently get no relief. When a bullied employee goes to human resources, what typically happens? HR turns to the legal department looking for guidance. The lawyers, whose job it is to protect the organization, play the legal card instead of the human card. For example, belittling an employee may be inappropriate and yet still within the letter of the law. In fact, **because most bullying is same-sex and not against a protected group, many bullying tactics are not illegal**. The organization in effect sides with the manager who now feels his/her actions and methods have been validated. In the future, as the concept of a "hostile environment" becomes more clearly defined, there may be more legal avenues for employees who are bullied. But for now, these employees are basically out of luck.

Finally, bullying often continues in organizations because front-line and mid-level managers believe that senior leaders condone or even approve of it. Some senior executives are bullies themselves, and you can bet they're not going to do anything about the problem. The Survey of Abusive Workplaces notes that 19 percent of the time, bullies followed either explicit or "understood" instructions from their boss. Most often though, these senior executives are simply tough-minded leaders whose directives are misinterpreted. Phrases like "Get tough with your people," "Don't show your weaknesses" and "Discipline those who need it" can easily be misconstrued by downline managers who are under pressure to produce results.

Bullies…never liked them, never will. I don't know what happened to the schoolyard bullies I knew as a kid. My hope is that they "grew up rather than just grew taller" as my friend Brian Gareau says. In other words, I hope they matured. Childhood bullying has received a lot of attention in recent years for being a key factor in the growing epidemic of school violence. Workplace bullying deserves a great deal more attention than it's getting, not just because of the cost to organizations, but because of the cost in human suffering.

How *You* Doin'?

There are two questions each of us must answer when it comes to workplace bullies:

1. Do we tolerate them? Do you witness bullying and look the other way? Are you aware that it's happening on your team or in another department and yet do nothing? When you stay silent, you are in effect siding with the bully.

2. Are we one of them? Do you routinely engage in any of the following behaviors:

- Intimidating a person either verbally or physically?
- Excluding or isolating someone socially or physically?
- Withholding necessary information or purposefully giving the wrong information?
- Yelling or using profanity?
- Criticizing a person constantly?
- Falsely accusing someone of "errors" not actually made?
- Starting, or failing to stop, destructive rumors or gossip about a person?
- Taking credit for work done by others?
- Abusing the evaluation process by lying about a person's performance?
- Using confidential information about a person to humiliate him/her privately or publicly?
- Assigning undesirable work as punishment?
- Making unreasonable demands of one person with respect to workload, deadlines or duties?
- Enjoying, even just a little bit, being able to control or dominate employees?

If you think you might be a bully, get some help. Contact

human resources or an outside counselor. Bullying is often a symptom of a deeper issue. Choosing to stop these behaviors will make those you work with happier, and you'll be happier too.

StreetSavvy Techniques

If you have even the slightest inkling that your employees may consider you a bully, I urge you to heed the following:

1. **Increase your self-awareness**. As you can tell from the list above, bullying is much broader than the threat of or actual physical violence. Realize that any intimidating or dominating behaviors, even if well intended, are not the reason for your success. Any success you've enjoyed has been despite these behaviors, not because of them. Over the long run, and especially as more young people enter the workforce, this leadership style will actually be detrimental to your success. Employees just won't stand (or stay) for it.

2. **Never use threats as a method to achieve desired results**. Suggesting to employees that they'll be given less-than-pleasant assignments or that they won't be promoted, allowed to take vacation or get salary increases would be considered threatening by most people. Of course, as a leader, you need to make employees aware of the logical consequences of their behavior, but threatening negative actions only corrupts the culture. Remember that a threat is in the eye (or gut, as the case may be) of the beholder, so check your choice of words, tone of voice and body language. If you sense any unease from employees when giving direction or asking questions, step back and evaluate your approach.

3. **Work diligently to put a stop to any bullies on your team**. Evaluate the leaders who report to you, if any, to determine if they use intimidating or harassing techniques. If they do and

you do nothing to stop it, employees will believe that you not only allow, but actually encourage, this approach. You become the bully's accomplice.

If any of your co-workers or your leader is a bully, look for opportunities to gently give them constructive feedback. Consider the possibility that they may not be aware of their behaviors and their effect on people. Early in my career, I worked for a CEO who was a bully. One day he called me in and asked me point-blank why everyone was afraid of him. When someone opens the door like that, have the courage to walk through it. Give him or her honest and constructive feedback.

Even if bullies don't invite feedback, you can still get your point across. Identify the business result that is most important to that person – such as customer service or quality or profit. Then, without suggesting they might be a bully, bring to their attention how their behaviors and actions negatively impact the result they most care about. Look for opportunities when they are frustrated about results and use it to broach the subject.

5

Let 'Em Know How *They* are Doin'... Deliver Painless Performance Appraisal

As kids, it seemed that no matter what we did, we were always getting "report cards." There were the usual report cards from school, but we also received feedback in many other forms that let us know how well we were performing in various areas of our lives. For example, in games and sports, our individual "report card" was the order in which we were chosen for the team and whether we played first or second string. The team's report card, of course, was the final score. There was even a subtle grading system involved with dates and parties.

But looking back, the most significant "report card" I got came from my dad each night when he arrived home from work. That was when he assessed how well I'd done that day in terms of homework, chores, behavior and attitude. It wasn't enough to simply do what needed to be done. He cared about *how* I said and did things.

My father's frequent and consistent appraisal of my performance kept me on the right track. If I'd been a wise guy with my grandmother that afternoon or had forgotten to take out the trash, you can bet he straightened me out in no uncertain terms. He knew if I was having trouble in math or slacking off in citizenship because we talked about school every night at the dinner table. As a result, my school report cards were anticlimactic.

As you might imagine, our dinner conversation was often quite lively. I remember frequently saying, "Yes, sir" between bites of spaghetti and meatballs. And more than a few times I left the table with agida. (Agida, pronounced *'ah-jih-da,* is Italian for heartburn or upset stomach.)

Some of my friends' parents weren't as on top of things as my dad was. They didn't talk about school much. Although their meals might have been more pleasant, my buddies often dreaded getting their school report cards because there were sure to be a few surprises for their parents and, as a result, a few consequences for them.

Surprises…uncertainty…unexpected feedback…consequences…

Perhaps those are the same reasons why many people are apprehensive or anxious about their performance appraisal – the "workplace report card." We don't like surprises and uncertainty when it comes to our performance reviews.

The most commonly used performance assessment methods – self-appraisal, 360-degree feedback, elaborate forms, simple forms – focus on one or two summary events each year. But any performance appraisal system worth its salt includes ongoing, regular feedback (a.k.a., your father's nightly dinner-table assessment). In other words, **employees shouldn't be surprised at review time.**

And yet, all too often they are.

Employees think they are doing reasonably well – at least no one has said anything to indicate otherwise – and then in the middle of the annual performance review, they find out there's a problem. It's like being blindsided by a truck. And it only has to happen once for employees to become wary of the entire review process.

Employees aren't the only ones not fond of performance appraisal. Over the years, scores of leaders have told me it's the least favorite part of their job – and that's putting it mildly! In my experience, the only performance appraisal systems leaders like are the ones they haven't used yet!

I'll bet a Philly cheesesteak that you're nodding your head in agreement and that you'd like to give me your perspective on the performance appraisal process. But until we meet in person and walk the streets of leadership together, let me tell you what I think.

Many leaders are frustrated with their organization's performance appraisal systems. Yes, that's right – system*s*, plural. Most organizations understand the inherent value and importance of performance appraisal. As a result, they are engaged in a never-ending quest for the "holy grail" of performance assessment. It seems that as soon as managers become familiar with the current assessment, the organization switches to something "better." Consequently, leaders spend their valuable time learning the mechanics of each system instead of investing time providing valuable feedback to employees.

Furthermore, performance appraisal systems are often voluminous and overwhelming. When I ask leaders how much time it takes them to complete performance reviews, they tell me they spend anywhere from 45 minutes to three hours gathering information and writing the review. The "sit down" as they call it, typically lasts from 15 minutes to an hour. Almost all of them say, "I try to get it over and done with as quickly as possible."

If your organization's policy is to conduct reviews on the anniversary of employees' hire date, it's not too bad because your work is spread out throughout the year. But if your organization requires that all reviews be done at the same time each year and you have a significant number of employees on your team, you could spend weeks completing forms and having meetings on top of the other pressing requirements of your job.

But there's a fascinating dichotomy with performance appraisal: what can be voluminous for leaders is often woefully inadequate for employees. Consider that **the typical employee works an average of 2000 hours a year, and yet we usually only spend between one and four hours a year reviewing and assessing that employee's performance!**

Am I the only one who sees a problem here? If I could give Corporate America what my father used to call "the back of my hand," perhaps more people would wake up to the importance and value of both formal performance appraisal and ongoing feedback.

Randy Pennington, business performance expert and author of *Results Rule!*, puts it this way: "Leaders assume that completing a form once or twice a year is providing feedback. Instead, it's more effective to think about performance appraisal in a different context. In bowling, for example, there is a final score but there is also ongoing, consistent feedback. Imagine bowling an entire game but not knowing your score until the end. That's how bowling would work if we applied the performance appraisal model. The employee throws a ball down the alley, it disappears through a sheet and the leader records the score on a clipboard. Who would want to play that game? And yet we wonder why employees and managers hate performance appraisal."

It seems to me that we could do away with a lot of the pain

Deliver Painless Performance Appraisal

and suffering associated with performance assessment if we as leaders would commit to giving employees ongoing performance feedback throughout the year...and then actually did it! It baffles me that otherwise smart leaders ignore the logical recommendation of giving regular feedback. To stay on track and be productive, team members must have frequent feedback as well as an annual report card.

One reason many leaders don't provide regular feedback is that they lack an understanding of how to give constructive feedback. I know these skills are described in performance appraisal instructions and taught with passion during performance appraisal training. But my experience has shown me that, like the assembly instructions that come with a child's toy, feedback instructions are often ignored. For some reason, leaders think they don't need those instructions in order to give effective feedback. (These are often the same leaders who don't understand why once-a-year reviews aren't having an impact on employee performance.)

Another reality is that plenty of leaders believe that employees don't want feedback, especially if it's negative or critical. I've found just the opposite to be true. When I give a presentation or facilitate a session on this topic, I typically ask the audience, "How many of you want to know where you stand with respect to how well you're doing your job?" Most people raise their hands. Then I ask, "How many of you want to know how you're doing, even if the feedback is negative?" Every time I ask that question, without exception, the response is larger and faster than to the first question. When I ask my final question, "Why?" people say things like, "So I can fix the problem" or "Because I don't want to be blindsided."

Most employees truly want to know where they stand when

it comes to their performance. What they don't want is to be surprised, belittled or brutalized in the process. The effectiveness of performance appraisal, as with so many other aspects of the people side of business, comes down to *how* it's done.

I realize that giving negative or constructive feedback can be uncomfortable, and I understand it's human nature to want to avoid an activity that we anticipate will be unpleasant. The irony is that performance assessment truly isn't unpleasant… *if it's done right!* The majority of feedback encounters should be positive since most employees' overall performance is acceptable. **When you don't provide regular feedback, you're missing a huge opportunity to reinforce solid performance.** And after all, isn't that what you want from employees – consistent, solid performance?

As for the few negative situations that will inevitably occur, if you deal with them when they first appear, there usually is very little discomfort involved. It's when you let problems fester and grow that you invite stress and major confrontation.

Perhaps if more leaders saw performance appraisal as a means to a better end – to better bottom-line results – instead of just one more thing they have to do, it could shed its maligned reputation and become the powerful tool it has the potential to be.

As a child and an adolescent, I was fortunate in that my parents acknowledged and reinforced my positive accomplishments. They also let me know – quickly, clearly and respectfully – when I wasn't performing to their expectations and guided me to improve. Honestly, I appreciated the feedback…the good and the bad (and sometimes even the ugly). It's clear to me now why I looked forward to my father coming through the door after a day at work…at least most nights.

Since most employees generally meet or exceed performance standards, performance assessment should primarily be an opportunity to provide positive reinforcement. Recognize and acknowledge positive performance every day, and your employees will be more satisfied and engaged. And who knows... someday they might even look forward to you "coming through the door."

How *You* Doin'
*when it comes to letting your people know how **they** are doin'?*

- ➢ Do you spend more time preparing employees' annual reviews than you do talking with them about their performance throughout the year?

- ➢ Do you rush through performance appraisal discussions, thereby missing even the once-a-year opportunity to provide effective performance feedback?

- ➢ Do you remember that effective feedback allows for and encourages comments from the employee?

StreetSavvy Techniques

1. Be clear in your descriptions of employees' job responsibilities and reinforce this in the way you give daily instructions. Clearly setting the benchmark or standard is the first step in appraising performance. The more clarity employees have, the more self-awareness they will develop and the better they will become at self-appraisal. You can help your leader do a better job of assessing your performance by clearly communicating your understanding of objectives and by providing results data.

2. Develop individualized feedback. For each member of your team, create a short, prioritized list (three to five items) of the areas for which you will give feedback. Because job responsibilities and requirements differ from employee to employee, feedback items will also differ. You can't provide effective feedback for every employee in all areas all the time, so focus on those areas that offer the most "bang for the buck" for each employee and position. Consider performance areas that contribute to the culture, bottom line or customer satisfaction (including internal customer satisfaction).

In addition, find out how each employee prefers to receive performance feedback – in writing, through casual conversation or perhaps in a more formal setting. The more comfortable employees are, the more engaged they will be in the feedback process.

Individualized feedback may sound like an administrative headache, but it is often actually easier for leaders and always much more relevant for employees. Job-specific assessments push the responsibility for performance appraisal from corporate HR down to those who are closest to the employees – the leaders, which is where it belongs anyway.

A number of years ago, I had an open-minded client that allowed me to steer the organization toward a performance appraisal system that measured different performance areas for different positions. For example, assessment items for a nurse's aide were different than those for a nurse which were different than the criteria for a nurse manager. This remarkable organization took the next step and connected job descriptions, hiring and selection criteria, recognition, coaching and even discipline to the same standards as the performance appraisal process. What a concept – accountability to the same standards from start to finish!

3. **Make frequent performance feedback for employees a priority.** You're likely stuck with your organization's performance appraisal process. And I know you're incredibly busy. So keep feedback quick and simple! Keep assessment forms for team members nearby at all times and make plenty of notes about their performance. This simple act not only reminds you and encourages you to provide regular feedback, but also shortens the time it takes to prepare forms for the annual review.

4. **Catch performance gaps early, before they become major issues.** Employees will appreciate the heads-up just as you would. And in the long run, dealing with problems early actually saves you time and trouble. Once problems become monster size, they take more time to resolve, the solutions are more complex and emotions run a lot higher. For more information on coaching for performance, see Chapter 16.

6

"Climb in My Window"... Leverage Generational Strengths

For much of my childhood, there were three different generations living together under one roof: my brother and me, my parents and my grandmother. We spent *a lot* of time together, but interestingly, we didn't know we had "generational challenges." Did we have disagreements due to generational differences? Of course! But one thing was always a constant – respect for one another. We valued the talents and abilities that each of us contributed to the family. My grandmother brought wisdom and lightheartedness. My parents provided guidance and direction, along with financial and emotional security. Even my brother and I had roles. We did chores and were expected to get "book knowledge" so that we could become more successful than our parents and grandparents.

The generational spread wasn't just confined to my home; it was evident in my neighborhood as well. Multiple generations lived together in very close proximity. As with the members of my family, neighbors valued other neighbors from different generations. We knew that each person had unique strengths, no matter which generation they belonged to. As a result, our neighborhood was a cohesive group of people who didn't let age get in the way of a good life. To thrive, we had to work together as a team.

An older woman down the block taught me music. A neighbor in his thirties helped the elderly man next door fix his roof. The 50-year-old proprietor of the local food store hired neighborhood teenage boys who needed to work to supplement their families' income. Children who needed to cross a busy intersection often asked adults (even strangers), "Will you cross me please?"

I vividly remember one of the important roles we kids filled in the neighborhood: climbing in neighbors' windows. Now, before you think our parents were preparing us for a life of crime, let me explain. There were some elderly neighbors on our street who frequently locked themselves out of their houses. Back then, there weren't deadbolts, and door locks didn't require keys. The doorknob had a button that you pushed in to lock, and it was easy to accidentally lock the door on your way out. The only way in was to climb through the window.

My friends and I would be on the front steps playing cards and eating polly seeds, or in the street in the middle of a heated game of Dead Box, when Mrs. Navasio or Mr. Trombetta would walk up and say, "Alex, (I was called Alex until I went to college) will you climb in my window please?" One of my buddies would boost me up to the first floor window, and I'd throw a leg over the windowsill and haul myself in. Then, very carefully, because

The door on the right is to my childhood home in South Philly. To the left is the neighbor's house and the actual window I climbed through many times during my youth.

there were always lots of knickknacks sitting around, I'd jump to the floor or step on a plastic-covered sofa or chair. I'd walk over and unlock the door, and there would be an appreciative Mrs. Navasio or Mr. Trombetta. To be honest, we didn't do it because we were especially thoughtful or altruistic kids. Climbing in windows was part of our contribution to the neighborhood team.

How about your "neighborhood"? Do your employees from different generations work together as a team? Do you value the strengths and perspectives each generation brings to the table?

Today in Corporate America there are as many as four generations working together: Matures (born 1925-1945), Baby Boomers (born 1946-1964), Gen Xers (born 1965-1981), and New Millennials (born 1982-2002). Never before have so many people from so many age groups been thrown together in the workplace in such a variety of ways. The "corporate ladder" has been flattened, if not torn apart. Baby Boomers in their sixties work alongside twenty-year-olds. Recent college graduates oversee employees old enough to be their parents. It's a workforce that leaders haven't seen before.

According to Cam Marston, author of *Motivating the "What's In It For Me?" Workforce*, Matures, Boomers, Gen Xers and New Millennials have vastly different perspectives on just about everything work-related, including:

- Reasons for working
- Definitions of success
- Work ethic
- Time
- Loyalty
- Technology
- Work-life balance
- Rewards for performance (such as titles and promotions)
- Meetings

- ➢ Respect
- ➢ Teams
- ➢ Definition of "Casual Friday"
- ➢ Excusable reasons for missing work

There is a need for understanding, empathy and mutual respect among people of different generations, more so than ever before. Instead, individuals in each generation tend to see themselves in the best light while seeing their co-workers from other generations in the worst light:

- ➢ **Matures** (5 percent of the workforce) are often perceived by the other generations as having no place in today's global, fast-paced, ever-changing, technology-based workplace. Even the Matures who occupy the top echelons of business are often considered "old school," their wisdom and experience passé.

- ➢ **Baby Boomers** (45 percent of the workforce) are quickly becoming the "new old-timers," and as a result, are often underutilized. Their majority in the ranks of corporate leadership, and therefore their power and control, is quickly slipping away. Younger generations tend to not listen to them and discount their value in the workplace.

- ➢ **Gen Xers** (40 percent of the workforce), who place a high value and emphasis on work-life balance, are often seen as unambitious and therefore a threat to the success and profitability of the organization. As more and more of them enter the leadership ranks, their work ethic is frequently questioned.

- ➢ **New Millennials** (10 percent of the workforce) often have a need for instant gratification and rapid promotion, which are viewed as unreasonable and unrealistic by

Leverage Generational Strengths

older-generation leaders. Other generations miss the opportunities inherent with a generation that values speed and results.

So what does all this mean for you, the leader?

It means that you have an incredibly challenging job! You must manage the extremely diverse attitudes, beliefs and worldviews of your employees. You must build and lead high-performing teams with members from four different generations who are essentially speaking different languages. Is this often frustrating? Yes. Is it worthwhile nonetheless? Absolutely! **In today's business climate, you *need* team members who think and act differently. You *want* employees with diverse skills, abilities and perspectives.**

Adding to your challenge is the fact that the 78 million Baby Boomers currently in the workforce are on their way out. Experts predict this will result in a 30 to 40 percent workforce shortfall in the not-so-distant future. That means you and your organization are going to have to get more serious and more creative about filling the void left by the Boomers. And it's not just a "body" void; it's a knowledge void, which can be far more devastating.

So what are organizations doing about these generational issues? Some, like hospitals, are doing a fairly good job of engaging all four generations because they have to. Patients – their customers – range in age from infants to the elderly. (How many industries can say the same about their customers? Very few.) Consequently, many hospitals are forming intergenerational teams and providing additional training and resources to build intergenerational empathy. They're also working to enhance their communication efforts to take into account generational style differences.

Most organizations, however, aren't as far down the generational-inclusion path. They may hold the occasional training program or distribute a few articles, but generational realities are rarely woven into the fabric of the organization. Why? First, because many top-level leaders mistakenly believe that generational issues do not have a negative impact on the bottom line, they don't place a high priority on addressing them. Second, many organizations have yet to realize that generational differences represent the next wave of diversity. I work with a number of diversity/inclusion experts who tell me that they see a lack of awareness about generational diversity and that too many organizations are still stuck with the notion that diversity is about ethnicity, religious preference or sexual orientation. Yet most of these same experts agree that generational issues are more encompassing and therefore have a potentially greater negative impact than traditional diversity issues.

The net effect is that leaders are often on their own when it comes to handling generational challenges. So what are you to do?

Perhaps the most crucial thing is to remember this: You're not going to change people, at least in any substantial way, so don't waste your time trying. Some diversity experts suggest having employees focus on the commonalities between themselves and their co-workers. I believe there will always be people who will never admit that they are similar to people of another generation – or of another ethnicity, race or gender for that matter. However, I think even the most closed-minded and stubborn person would be willing to admit that someone of a different generation has some characteristic or strength that benefits the team and the organization.

So focus on inclusion, not diversity (i.e., differences.) Direct your energy and attention to harnessing the positive qualities of each generational group. Commit to building a generation-friendly culture by fostering respect among employees. Leveraging existing strengths and tendencies is much more practical – not to mention easier – than attempting to change people's personalities.

Maximizing the positives that come from generational inclusion can lead to professional – and even personal – satisfaction. Personally, you'll have more positive human encounters and better relationships. Professionally, you'll be able to attract, engage and retain a wide variety of talented people for your team who are willing to "climb in each other's windows" and help each other succeed. Intergenerational goodwill produces a tremendous payoff in teamwork, productivity and profitability, and has a significant impact on an organization's ability to beat the competition, achieve solid financial results and build a reputable employer brand.

How *You* Doin'?

- Do you have a handle on your current generational mix – do you know how much of your workforce falls into each generation? Awareness is always the best place to start…and the numbers may just surprise you.

- Are you aware of your personal prejudices and negative stereotyping of people from other generations? (We all do it to some extent.)

- Do the people who work with you and for you talk positively or negatively about others from different generations?

- Do you consistently remind others (and yourself) of the positive character traits of other generations and the reasons why it's important to acknowledge them?

StreetSavvy Techniques

1. **Get educated**. I'm going to give you the "straight skinny," as we say in Philadelphia: this topic is critical to your success as a leader. I recommend you read and study the books *Motivating the "What's In It For Me?" Workforce* by Cam Marston and *Generations Working Together: What Everyone Needs to Know and Do* by Laura Bernstein. You can find them at bookstores or www.ADLAssociates.com.

2. **Come to terms with your own generational realities**. You belong to one of these four generations, and that means your perspectives are likely different from the perspectives of your manager, your team and your colleagues. While employees might be able to get away with discounting their co-workers from different generations, leaders don't have that luxury. If you intend to be successful, you must learn to lead, motivate and leverage the strengths of employees from all generations.

3. **Build understanding and respect**. Awareness is the first step to helping your employees appreciate others' strengths and talents. Get your team together and make a list of the positive attributes of each generation. Then ask each team member to privately write down on a piece of paper how many of these attributes exist in the people they work with – both on the team and outside the team. This is a great exercise for building awareness and providing recognition across generational lines.

    Next, ask every team member to define the word "respect" and then share their definitions with the group. Why? Because this is something people of all ages want, and yet the way one shows respect differs greatly from generation to generation. For example, Baby Boomers feel respected when working collaboratively on a team toward an objective.

Gen Xers feel respected when left alone to develop ideas. Because one person's good intentions can inadvertently lead to someone else feeling disrespected, share all the definitions with everyone on the team to encourage generational understanding.

4. Put newfound understanding and respect into action. Make a concerted effort to put people of different generations together on projects or teams. Working together in close proximity and toward a common goal will help team members put into action the understanding, empathy and respect for one another that they've recently discovered. Be sure to recognize not only the results and outcomes of these activities, but also the cooperative efforts.

7

Utilize Street Specialists...
Practice "Right Fit" Leadership

Not long ago, I took a business trip to my hometown of Philadelphia. With my client meeting over, I had a few hours to kill before heading to the airport. I didn't need a watch to tell me it was lunchtime, so I headed down to South Philly where I grew up, knowing I'd find plenty of great places to eat. After downing a cheesesteak or two (what the heck – I don't get back to Philly that often), I pointed my rental car toward the old neighborhood.

The narrow streets were more difficult to navigate than I remembered, but I finally reached Hutchinson, the street I grew up on. As I glanced down the block, I could see in an instant I'd never find a place to park. The streets in that part of Philly are so narrow you can only park on one side of the street, leaving barely enough room for cars to get by.

Recent shot of Hutchison Street in South Philadelphia where I grew up.

I parked the car a few blocks away and started walking. Although the stores had all changed and a few buildings had been torn down, surprisingly, the neighborhood looked much like it did all those years ago. As I walked, I started to think about the guys who used to roam these streets with me. There were five of us in our group of close friends, and we all lived within three blocks of one another. As I passed the houses where they had lived, each one of my friends came to mind.

There was Joe, who always seemed to have an attractive young lady on his arm. (He got girls for the rest of us, too!) As you might guess, his specialty was flirting, and he was the only boy I knew who actually liked girls from a very early age.

Frank was the best driver in our group and the only one with a car, so he took us everywhere we went.

Ted, by far the most gifted athlete among us, was always the first one picked when we chose teams for our street games. He could catch anything, even a soggy football. (We used newspapers tied with string for footballs. If that makes you feel sorry for us, don't. We had a lot of fun.)

Danny always carried a sharp pocketknife and had a steady hand. His "job" was to cut the pimple balls in half for our games of Halfball.

And then there was me. I was the diplomat with the interpersonal skills – the one who talked to the parents when we stepped out of line or didn't get home in time. Maybe I was destined to become a speaker and consultant….

These guys, each with their own strengths and talents, were my earliest exposure to "right fit" – matching a person's skills with a particular task. We were, in effect, "Street Specialists." We weren't consciously aware of using the right person for the job, but we practiced it nonetheless.

You'd think the right-fit concept would be common sense to adults...but you'd be wrong. In all the years I've spent as an employee, manager, corporate executive, consultant and executive coach, the most common situation I encounter in organizations is this: people with few or no leadership skills working in leadership positions. When it comes to leadership, it seems "right fit" has gone right out the window.

If I add the title "M.D." to my business card, it doesn't make me a medical doctor. And yet every year, the title of "leader" is given to tens of thousands of people in organizations around the world who don't have effective leadership skills. The result is *wrong* fit – people who are leaders in name only.

Don't get me wrong. Most of these people are hard-working, get-the-job-done men and women with exceptional technical skills. In fact, that's often the very reason they are promoted to leadership positions. They are such valuable employees and critical intellectual assets that the organization doesn't want to risk losing them. So they are promoted into supervisory roles as a reward for their technical performance.

When you combine this right person/wrong fit scenario with an unwillingness on the part of senior management to hold leaders accountable for effectively leading *their* people, you have the makings of a serious problem: individuals allowed to *stay* in leadership roles even though they have a negative impact (or neutral at best) on the people who report to them. Ineffective leaders become unfortunate role models for up-and-coming managers, and the lack of true leadership continues from "generation to generation."

How can organizations that genuinely believe in making effective business decisions let something like leadership inadequacy continue? The answer is complex, but the core issue is that they fail to fully understand the negative impact of poor leadership on business results and the long-term health of the organization. Why? Because there is no INI. No, it's not a type of belly button; it stands for **Immediately Noticeable Impact.**

Technical skills typically have an Immediately Noticeable Impact on results. As long as the widgets are produced, the sales are made and the beans are counted, "leaders" keep their jobs. Leadership skills and effectiveness, on the other hand, often don't have an Immediately Noticeable Impact on results. Their effect is significant but subtle, direct but longer term. A recent Gallup survey of 1.5 million employees concluded that leaders profoundly affect – positively or negatively – employee attitudes and engagement and therefore productivity, customer loyalty, safety and, ultimately, the organization's profitability. Organizations that promote and retain leaders with excellent technical skills but poor people skills often achieve short-term results while sabotaging lasting success.

Back in Philly, we didn't put a kid who couldn't catch the ball in the position of catcher. And if we picked the wrong guy to "go long" in our football game, we saw the impact right away and made adjustments before the next play. But with leadership deficiencies, problems may not show up for weeks, months or even years. For example, many organizations with ongoing customer service challenges never make the connections to ineffective leadership. And yet there's often a direct cause-and-effect relationship: a manager with poor leadership skills causes employees to become disengaged and disinterested in providing excellent service.

Research tells us that, for the most part, people leave their leaders, not their organizations. Surveys state that it costs one-fifth to one-third of an employee's salary to replace that individual. A leader who runs off three team members each making $60,000 a year costs the organization between $36,000 and $60,000 to hire and retrain their replacements – a direct, bottom-line financial impact. The effects of poor leadership don't show up overnight, but rather over the course of time. It's a subtle effect that has a dramatic impact, especially when you consider this example represents just one of many leaders in an organization! Organization wide, the financial impact would be in the hundreds of thousands if not millions of dollars.

It's no secret that the demand for workers in the future will far outpace the supply. Attracting and retaining qualified workers will be critical to success. Will salary, benefits and corporate culture be crucial? Yes. But all the research indicates that leaders are the number one factor in worker satisfaction. In his book *First Break All the Rules*, Marcus Buckingham says that front-line leaders are the key to attracting and retaining talented employees. That means that **leadership skills trump everything else when it comes to retention.**

I know what some of you are saying: "Al, we put all our new leaders through leadership development training, and existing leaders have the opportunity to attend ongoing leadership development training throughout the year." Okay. I hear you. But guess what?

It isn't working!

Employee surveys continue to indicate that *despite the millions of dollars being spent on leadership development every year*, leaders still aren't as focused on the people side of business as they should be. And my experiences with organizations across the country lead me to believe that, *despite the millions of dollars being spent on leadership development every year,* leaders themselves are frustrated because they still don't have practical answers to their daily people challenges.

Fortunately, we can do something about the issue of in-name-only leaders. Leadership and people skills are not like natural athletic giftedness that one is either born with or without. They can be learned and improved upon. That doesn't mean that becoming a better leader is easy, but it is very doable. The good news about leadership skills is that they don't have to be perfect or even excellent. They just need to be better than they have been. It's all about continuous improvement. (Here's a little known truth: You don't have to be a phenomenal leader to be better than most of the other leaders out there!)

Technical people can be high performing leaders *if* they get support – effective training, timely feedback and quality coaching and mentoring. They are proven performers who typically have earned the respect of their co-workers. They were able to grow their technical competence; they can certainly develop leadership ability as well.

More and more organizations are coming to this realization that their technical superstars need dedicated help if they are to become superior leaders. Two such client organizations – one that might be thought of as "old fashioned" and another that many would assume to be bureaucratic – are quite StreetSavvy when it comes to helping technically strong employees make the transition into leadership.

A public utility in Florida assigns qualified, experienced leaders to mentor new managers and to coach them specifically on people issues. A heavy equipment manufacturer has come to understand that reinforcement is the key to leadership development. This organization follows up all of its training with additional workshops that strengthen previously introduced concepts and provide leaders with the opportunity to work through real workplace issues. Still another client utilizes an external executive coach (yours truly) for one-on-one coaching with leaders so that those who are comfortable dispatching trucks can be equally comfortable providing recognition or giving a performance review.

So what's the YROI (*Your* Return on Investment) for developing *your* leadership skills and becoming a Street Specialist? Why should you bother?

- ➤ **More influence.** As someone with exceptional technical skills, you likely have a great deal of technical influence. However, if your leadership skills aren't up to par, the level of respect others have for you will likely suffer. Becoming a people expert will put you head and shoulders above other leaders and help you garner leadership influence.

- ➤ **Less overtime**. Better leadership skills mean less turnover. Period. Less turnover means less time you have to spend selecting and training new employees, and less time your team has to work late to cover the tasks that don't get done while the position is empty. Less time at work means more time for life outside of work.

- ➤ **Continued success**. If you (as an individual or an organization) don't focus on and develop leadership skills, you're simply shooting yourself in the foot. You may have gotten by or even achieved some measure of success up to this point, but I guarantee that you won't be able to sustain that success into the future without effective leadership skills.

As kids, we inherently understood the value of being Street Specialists. Matching tasks with individual skills and abilities ensured that as a group we were able to do more than we could have individually. But that involved kids' games and street sports, where there wasn't much at stake.

Today, organizations depend on maximum performance from their people but don't seem to pay much attention to putting the best leaders in leadership positions. If more leaders and organizations would commit to Right Fit Leadership, I believe they, too, could win more of their "games." Those who lead other leaders have a tremendous opportunity to have a significant impact on the leadership culture of an organization. Take that responsibility seriously and use your influence to create positive change.

How *You* Doin' as a leader?

- Are *you* a Street Specialist? Are your leadership skills the right fit for your position?

- Has the quest for positive, short-term results clouded your judgment about your long-term success as a leader of people?

- Do you take leadership development seriously, giving it as much focus and attention as staying proficient with your technical skills?

How *You* Doin' as a leader of leaders?

- Do you provide *effective* (defined as "capable of bringing about results" by *Merriam-Webster*) leadership training? Do you follow up to ensure that leaders understand and actually apply new concepts and skills? Do you provide qualified, caring mentors to new leaders?

> How are leaders promoted in your organization? Is it based primarily on technical skills and dollar orientation or on both technical and leadership skills?

> Do you truly hold leaders accountable for developing leadership skills and focusing on the people side of business? What are the consequences for those who don't?

StreetSavvy Techniques

Great technical skills are important, but they won't carry you through the many tough challenges of leadership. That will take solid leadership skills.

1. **Seek ongoing coaching, training and education in the areas of leadership and human interactions.** Virtually every individual experiences atrophy in the leadership zone. Just as muscles atrophy if they're not constantly used, so do leadership skills. Effective leadership development requires an ongoing, consistent effort. Find a leadership mentor, even if you have to go outside your organization, and counsel with him/her regularly. Share your people issues and concerns with your mentor as they occur, listen to his/her advice and then *apply* what you learn.

2. **Interact with your team members in a positive manner on a daily basis.** Remember, what's in your heart and in your head – your good leadership intentions – is not enough. You have to "walk the talk" and take action with your words and behaviors. Look for Immediately Noticeable Impact – notice how much more engaged your employees are and how much better they perform when you practice and apply good leadership skills.

And if you are a leader of leaders…

1. Evaluate your culture to discover the truth about your organization's leadership quotient. Pay close attention to employee comments from both climate surveys and casual conversations that indicate dissatisfaction with the leadership skills of their managers. Listen for comments from leaders about the unimportance of people skills. Take note if there's a lack of people-issue discussions. And of course, watch for the outright mistreatment of employees.

2. Include leadership skills as an important criterion for the selection and promotion of new managers. Many organizations say that people are their most important asset but continue to select and promote individuals with inadequate leadership skills. One of our key responsibilities as a leader is to practice Right Fit Leadership and put the best person in each position. When we hire or promote leaders under us who don't possess demonstrated leadership skills, we are failing in our responsibilities and not being personally accountable. (There's that accountability issue again!) If people see that leadership skills won't get them ahead in your company, they will develop a "why bother" mentality. When you have responsibility for, or influence over, the selection of a new leader, resist the temptation to let technical skills trump people skills – give them at least equal weight.

3. Regularly assess leaders' performance on the leadership aspects of their job. In other words, **evaluate *how* they achieve results**. Actions always speak louder than words, and what gets measured will get done. Require training, coaching or mentoring for leaders who demonstrate the need for help with interpersonal skills. For more StreetSavvy Techniques for performance assessment and coaching, see Chapters 5 and 16, respectively.

8

Take a Tip From the Butcher Shop Ladies... Use the Power of Influence

I learned about the power of influence at the Butcher Shop.

Supermarkets weren't common in the 50s and 60s, at least not in South Philly. You bought your meat at the Butcher Shop, your milk, eggs and fruit from vendors who came down the street, and the rest of your groceries from the little neighborhood market.

My mom usually went to the Butcher Shop twice a week. It was on 10th Street, about a block from our house. When I was young, I'd go with her to pick up pork chops, veal cutlets and braciole. I was amazed by the sheer size of the long, tall refrigerated-counter that stretched from one side of the room to the other. In front of that counter, lined up in an orderly fashion, would be

Cappuccio's Meat Market in South Philadelphia.

"The Ladies" – other women from the neighborhood who had also come to buy meat. They all dressed similarly – typically a housecoat with brightly colored flowers, no matter the time of year.

As my mom stood in line, I'd press my nose up against the glass counter. I'd stare at the spread of fresh seafood and the peppered slabs of meat, and listen to The Ladies talk, as Italian women tend to do. A lady at the front might tell the woman next to her about her daughter's upcoming wedding, and another woman down the line would chime in with her opinion about the band or the cake at her best friend's cousin's son's wedding.

True to South Philly, the Butcher Shop Ladies weren't afraid to tell it like it was…to tell everyone in the shop, for example, that a certain insurance company downtown would cheat you if you weren't careful. And they certainly weren't afraid to confront the butcher. They watched him like a hawk, making sure he gave them the best piece of meat and that he didn't put his thumb on the scale to add a bit of weight as he calculated the cost.

As a kid, I thought nothing special of the Butcher Shop Ladies. How could I know they wielded such power and influence in our neighborhood?

Now, my mother, Marion, was a StreetSavvy woman. She was strong-willed and opinionated, and she certainly wasn't afraid to speak her mind. Her friends turned to her for help and advice. She was nobody's fool, and she wasn't about to let anyone take advantage of her. (I can still remember how she handled the egg vendor who came whistling down our street once a week. He knew better than to leave a cracked egg at our house…knew that if he did, my mother would chase him down and make him replace it. I can picture him in my mind – standing there at our front door, a look of concern on his face, as my mother checked the eggs one by one. I'd be willing to bet that he kept a spare egg tucked delicately in his pocket, just in case.)

When I was younger, I believed that all of Mom's opinions and perspectives were solely her own and that no one could tell her anything. She didn't strike me as the type of person who was easily influenced. However, as I got a bit older, I discovered this wasn't always true. I was probably 12 years old when I mustered the courage one day to ask her how she came to the conclusion that Wildwood, New Jersey was the best place for our upcoming family vacation. Preparing my father's lunch pail, she turned to look at me and said, "The ladies at the Butcher Shop," as if all their husbands worked for the local travel agency.

Once that door was opened, she used the phrase often to reveal her source of influence. What I realize now, many years later, is that no woman waiting for a pound of ground beef could ever tell my mother what to do, but they influenced her just the same.

In the same way that the Butcher Shop Ladies influenced my mom, the people and culture of South Philly influenced my values, personality and view of the world. Of course, those with authority – like my parents and the police – influenced the way I acted, but there were other influencers that also affected the choices I made. These more subtle influencers included relatives, friends, teachers, TV, books, music, sports and hormones, just to name a few.

Non-authority influencers still shape my life today. The people I respect, the books I read, even my children (when I remember to listen to their developing wisdom) influence my decisions and choices. These influencers have no more authority over me than the Butcher Shop Ladies had over my mother, yet they affect everything I do personally, professionally and socially.

The reality is that each of us – including you – is influenced by people, situations and circumstances, every single day, whether we realize it or not. We hear a lot about the power of influence in politics, religion and social situations, but we don't hear much about the power of influence in business. Instead, it appears to be more in vogue to complain about a lack of authority. I often hear from frustrated managers (at all levels) that they "don't have the authority" to make certain decisions, demand specific behaviors, take disciplinary action, or buy necessary equipment and supplies.

I think these are valid concerns, but I also think there's something else – something deeper – going on. I think leaders are frustrated because they can't force employees to be engaged. We can often make employees do the basics of the job, but we can't make them give discretionary effort, nor can we force them to be committed or to have a good attitude.

Authority will get you bare minimum. It won't get you discretionary effort, but *influence* will!

It seems to me that too many leaders completely ignore the power of influence. They don't understand that influence is far more powerful than authority. Why? Because **authority leads to compliance, whereas influence leads to *commitment*.** Authority grabs employees' minds; influence captures their hearts. You can't force employees to be committed or engaged, but you can constantly *influence* them to be both.

For some situations, such as meeting production or sales quotas, having authority over people to force them to perform at a certain level can lead to better results…*short term*. But in the long run, overused authority in the workplace breeds resentment and disengagement. With today's multigenerational workforce, influence will win over authority every time. Older generations grew up in a more authoritarian culture and environment;

therefore they're accustomed to that type of management. Younger generations, however, push back against authority…and they push back hard.

Influence works with everyone *regardless* of age, gender, ethnicity or position. I'll take influence over authority any day!

Here's something else to think about: Once we allow ourselves and others to say, "I'm helpless because I don't have the authority," it's a slippery, downward slope. If we think we don't have the authority to do something, we won't take responsibility for the results. On the other hand, when we recognize the power of influence, we realize that we can – and must – hold ourselves accountable for results whether we have authority or not.

I can hear you now, saying, "Yeah right! How am I supposed to influence situations over which I have no authority or control?" Great question! Negotiation and mediation expert Linda Swindling says, "Even if you don't have the authority to make a decision, you *always* have the power to influence it." Let's look at the employee-selection process as an example. Although you may not have authority over the process, you can still have a tremendous impact on the selection of a co-worker, a fellow leader or even an upline leader. How? Start by proactively providing the person responsible for recruitment with relevant information about the position, such as job responsibilities, essential personality traits, and specific challenges the new individual may face. In addition, you can offer to assist with the interviewing process so that your input and feedback will be considered in the final decision. It's really no different than the Butcher Shop Ladies influencing my family's vacation plans.

As an executive coach and consultant, influence has been my best tool to get clients to move in a positive direction. I can't force a client to do anything (except maybe pay me by using vague threats about my Uncle Guido who's in the cement business). I've had to rely on relationships, respect and a proven track record. Over time, as my credibility has grown with clients, so has my influence. Likewise, I have no authority over you. But hopefully, through candor, sound recommendations and "ah-ha" moments, I can influence you to change some of your beliefs about leadership and help you to implement some different strategies.

As a leader, you must get work done *through* other people. To get results, you must become an influencer. Period. That's the YROI – influence consistently produces more positive, permanent results than authority, making your job easier.

Like most people, when I was a teenager, I resisted authority. On the other hand, I don't ever remember resenting being influenced. I did the right thing most of the time anyway, but I was so much more engaged when **I chose** to do what I felt was right for me. You might think that's just part of being a teenager – that teenagers will always prefer to make their own decisions rather than being dictated to. But *I believe that's true of humans at any age!* Your team members will be more engaged when they *choose* to do something because you influenced them rather than told them.

Have I influenced your thinking on this subject without reaching out from the pages and grabbing you by the shirt? I hope so. When someone grabbed your shirt in my old neighborhood, it was usually followed by an aggressive, "You talkin' to me?!"

When you think about it, it almost doesn't even matter whether you have the authority to do something or not because **even when you have authority, influence is always the better choice**. Take a tip from the Butcher Shop Ladies and use the power of influence to achieve lasting results.

How *You* Doin'?

> Who and what affects the decisions and choices you make in life? How many of those influencers have authority or control over you? (My guess is very few other than the government and the IRS.)

> Which do you believe is more powerful – influence or authority? Which do you respond to more positively?

> Would others say you are an influencer or an authoritarian?

> *Who or what can you positively influence that you don't currently have authority over?*

StreetSavvy Techniques

1. **Adopt the belief today that you do have influence** and then see how far your influence can go. For example, you may have the authority to send one of your direct reports on a business trip to a regional office. Instead of telling him to pack his bags, discuss the challenges in that particular office and ask how he thinks those issues might best be resolved. Chances are, he will come to the conclusion that he needs to deal with the problem in person. On the other hand, he might offer a solution that's even better. Either way, he'll be much more engaged and committed to the assignment because he came to the conclusion on his own.

2. **Earn the trust and confidence of your team members so they'll be receptive to your influence**. Think about the people who influence you and mimic their positive traits and characteristics. Treat people with respect and empathy. If you build a relationship, people will be open to your advice. And

the better you know someone, the more you'll know about how to influence that person.

You can maximize your influence when you genuinely keep others' best interests at heart. Help people see how changing their performance, productivity, attitude, or even their attire will benefit their career and/or personal life. Identify and share what's in it for them.

3. **Use the power of recognition and coaching to increase your influence.** Feedback and coaching are some of the most powerful ways to increase your influence. For example, let's say one of your salespeople doesn't dress appropriately. Reinforce what is considered appropriate by genuinely complimenting her when she wears something acceptable. If you do this consistently, she will eventually accept your constructive criticism on those occasions when she shows up inappropriately dressed.

Both positive reinforcement and constructive criticism send the message to employees that you care and that you will not let them fail or be hurt professionally. Think about it…who has influence over you? People who give you only negative feedback or no feedback at all? Or those who care enough about you to keep you out of trouble while supporting your strengths?

9

Join A Gang...
Model Your Employer Brand

As a teenager, I was part of a tight-knit "gang" of friends. We thought we were "cool." We walked with a certain swagger that we thought made us appear as if we were higher on the socioeconomic ladder than we actually were. We wore jeans and T-shirts with the sleeves rolled up in the summer (some guys kept their cigarettes there) and stuffed our hands in our pockets in the winter because gloves were *not* cool. We definitely had a different look than our peers in the suburbs.

But our group identity was more about values and priorities than looks. Although we certainly had our share of fun, we were not carousing troublemakers. Good grades were important to us, and we worked hard at school, but we weren't nerds. Most of us were either Italian or Jewish and proud of our heritage and ethnic traditions (especially the food). We had a deep respect for family, and perhaps most importantly, we were tenaciously loyal to each other.

We were proud of our group and the opportunity to be a part of it. Although we didn't realize we had our own "brand," that's what it was. Our brand gave us a common identity, a shared purpose and a strong sense of belonging.

The desire to belong is a fundamental human need. It's one of the reasons why humans throughout history have banded together in families, tribes and nations. Humans in the 21st century are no different. We belong to families, clubs, social groups, professional associations and religious institutions. And since most of us spend about a third of our waking hours at work, we want to feel that we belong there, too.

In talking with hundreds, if not thousands, of people each year, I find that many employees don't feel a sense of belonging to or connection with their organizations. Although there are a number of reasons for this disconnect, I think one of the most significant is that organizations don't make it a priority to promote their culture through employer branding.

Product branding or *external branding* is commonly described as the process of building a favorable image for a product that differentiates it in the minds of prospects and end users from other competitors. **Employer branding or internal branding is the process of building a favorable image or identity for an organization's culture that differentiates it, in the minds of current and prospective employees, from other organizations.**

While product branding revolves around customers' needs and wants, employer branding focuses on what employees need and want. But a first-class employer brand is more encompassing than wages, benefits and work environment. It also highlights how an organization puts its values about people into action in the workplace. Employer branding is about creating and effectively communicating a tangible picture of what it's like to work for a company. It is, in essence, packaging the organizational culture for mass consumption.

I find it ironic that nearly all companies have learned – or at least are aware of – the power of product branding and how critical it is to long-term success. And yet there seems to be little appreciation for the significance of employer branding and its impact on the bottom line. But high-performance organizations recognize that employer branding and profit are connected. (Is it difficult to measure the effects of employer branding on the bottom line? Absolutely! Does that mean it doesn't have a significant impact? Absolutely not!) These companies understand that if they can create a cultural identity that is unique, refreshing and appealing to their ideal prospective employees, they'll have qualified candidates lined up at their doors begging to work for them. (Think Yahoo!, Google and the early days of Microsoft.)

To those who say, "We're concerned first about what our customers think and then what our employees think," I say, "You've got it backward…it should be the other way around." Solid employer branding leads to solid product and service branding. If you create an exceptional experience for your employees, they'll do the same for your customers.

Starbucks, for example, is more than a great cup of coffee, just as Southwest Airlines is more than a low-cost mode of transportation. People make the difference in these product brands, and the people are a reflection of the employer brand. In cases like these, the organization's culture becomes such an integral part of the organization's presence in the marketplace that the two can't be separated. When consumers make their daily Starbucks run, no matter which location they visit, they expect to be served by a certain type of individual: coffee-savvy, engaging, free-spirited. Likewise, people who take a Southwest flight expect a casual, friendly, fun experience that's very different than what they'd have on most other major airlines.

Because these organizations' cultures are so tightly intertwined with their product brands, their employer brands have become familiar to the general public. As a result, individuals who share the same characteristics are attracted to these organizations, producing an inflow of prospective employees who are a match with the culture. It's pre-selection at its best, as if there's an unstated rule that says, "If you're not in sync with our employer brand, don't bother applying." These new, in-sync employees continue to feed and enhance the employer brand, within both the organization and the marketplace, creating an ongoing positive cycle that feeds on itself. Conversely, organizations that lack a distinct employer brand often hire people who aren't a good cultural match, diluting the culture, costing the company money and negatively impacting the product brand.

Lest you think employer branding is relevant only for large, consumer-centric organizations, let me tell you about a small, privately-held company of which I was one of the owners. Although we didn't call it employer branding, we developed a well-defined corporate culture. Maintaining that culture was such a priority that "organizational fit" carried the same weight as technical skills when it came to selecting new employees. Once candidates met the technical criteria, they were interviewed by no less than three employees from various levels in the organization to determine if they were in sync with our culture. If the consensus was that an applicant didn't complement us, he or she was not offered a position, no matter how well-qualified otherwise.

The result was a stable organizational culture comprised of committed, engaged individuals. As with most companies, we experienced a few lean years here and there. During those times, employees voluntarily took short-term pay cuts *and* worked weekends to help us get back on track. This is just one example of what author Rita Bailey describes in her book *Destination Profit: Creating People-Profit Opportunities in Your Organization* when she says, "What sustains a business, regardless of what's happening outside, is the right culture." A well-established employer brand produces a secure internal environment that enables employees to remain focused on business despite ever-changing external factors such as competition, technology, customer requirements and economic conditions.

Successful employer brands have three common characteristics:

1. **Clarity** – The power of an internal brand comes from clear, concise, descriptive statements. There's little value in an employer brand if it takes more than 10 to 20 seconds to describe or if it's so vague that it is, in effect, meaningless.

2. **Candor** – Your employer brand must ring true. Beyond the initial sound bite, you should have a description that addresses both the good and the bad that employees will face. People are smart. They know work won't be "fun," "creative" and "supportive" all the time. They want to know up front what the realities are – hard work, challenges from competitors, demanding customers, government regulations, etc. Give it to them straight, and they'll be less likely to react negatively when the inevitable frustrations occur.

3. **Appeal** – This is probably the most essential element. A successful employer brand paints a picture that people want to be part of. We sometimes forget the basics, like what's in it for employees. Who cares if your brand is clear and honest if it doesn't *resonate with employees?* (How do you know what's meaningful to employees? Ask them!) People want to work for an organization they can be proud of – one that is financially stable, provides quality products and services, and respects and appreciates its employees.

You'll know your employer brand is effective when it has "legs" – the kind of legs that walk the talk – when employees at all levels of the organization exemplify the brand through their attitudes, behaviors and actions, day in and day out.

Several years ago, one of my clients decided to clarify and upgrade its already positive employer brand. This organization understands that employer branding is a journey that never ends. Their commitment to continuous improvement paid off when, a few years into the process, one of their executives gave a speech. Afterward, two people approached her and said, "You don't know us, but we work for one of your customers. We want you to know that your employees act exactly the way you described your culture." What a testimony to this company's efforts and the importance of employer branding!

Perhaps you're thinking, "Sounds great, Al. I'm onboard with the concept. But what does employer branding have to do with me? It's an HR issue."

Actually, employer branding is a leadership issue. No program, process or initiative will be effective over the long term without the support of all levels of leadership, and employer branding is no exception.

Leaders bring the employer brand to life, just as they do with product and service brands. They are responsible for clarifying the brand for their teams and for modeling the characteristics of the brand. According to Libby Sartain, former Chief Human Resources Officer for Yahoo! and Southwest Airlines, "Employees look to leaders to be the ultimate expression and representation of what they consider the [employer] brand to stand for." I would add that **leaders are the living examples of what the employer brand *really* stands for** regardless of what is printed in the annual report or said in executive speeches.

So what's in it for you to support your employer brand? Or, if your organization doesn't yet have an employer brand, why should you champion the cause to develop one? What's the YROI?

- **Better results.** When your actions are in sync with the employer brand, you build trust with team members. The more you and other leaders model the brand, the more employees trust the organization as a whole. Employees who trust their leaders and their organization are more engaged and more likely to give discretionary effort, which leads to better results.

- **Better people**. An established employer brand is a tremendous asset in recruitment and retention. Better applicants means you can be more selective in your hiring practices, which means the best employees end up on *your* team. And that makes your job a whole lot easier!

As I learned in my youth, belonging to a group where one feels comfortable, accepted, valued and respected meets a powerful human need. Whether your employer brand is characterized by fun, creativity, stability or conservatism doesn't really matter. Your employer brand stands for what's special about your "gang." When you get clear about your employer brand and start sharing it with the world, you'll discover droves of wonderful people who are just like you and who want to join your gang.

How *You* Doin'?

- Does your organization have a defined, clearly communicated employer brand?
- Do you consistently model the positive attributes of your employer brand or organizational culture?

➢ What would most of your employees say if asked, "What's it like where you work?"

StreetSavvy Techniques

If your organization has an employer brand...

1. **Model the attributes of your employer brand.** You are the connector between the officially stated employer brand and what happens on a daily basis on the front lines. If your employer brand doesn't ring true at every level of the organization, you're almost asking for disengagement.

2. **Leverage your brand.** Use it in recruiting, selection and promotion. Reinforce the brand throughout every aspect of your operations. Look for and capitalize on every opportunity to recognize employee behaviors that support the brand. Consider your brand when completing performance appraisals and when coaching or giving feedback. Employees (and leaders, for that matter) should be evaluated on how well they support the brand.

3. **Ensure your team connects with the organization's employer brand.** Because an employer brand is somewhat broad-based, you must help your team identify which aspects of the brand most resonate with them. For example, marketing-department creative types might be drawn to different characteristics of the brand than the more left-brained members of the accounting department. Furthermore, operational realities vary by department, and consequently, so does the application of the brand. If you fly on Southwest Airlines a few times, you'll observe that both pilots and flight attendants exhibit the corporate culture of fun, but in different ways.

4. Create an internal buzz about your brand to help current employees understand and appreciate their group identity. Then utilize them as ambassadors of the brand to spread the word to outsiders, including prospective employees, customers and vendors.

And if your organization doesn't yet have an employer brand...

1. Package and promote the positive aspects of your culture. Every organization has cultural standards; some are simply better defined and communicated than others. Maximize what you've got by asking your team members to identify which characteristics of your corporate culture are the most meaningful for them. Then look for ways to apply those traits throughout your operation.

2. Develop a team brand that supports the overall organizational message. A team brand will produce the same benefits as an employer brand but on a smaller scale. A solid team brand will earn your group a reputation as *the* place to work in your organization. Involve your employees in developing a brand for your group, team or department (within the confines of your organizational culture, of course). There are many opportunities for employee involvement, but creating a brand for the people side of your business is without a doubt one of the most important. If you want maximum return from your brand, it's imperative that you listen to and incorporate feedback from your people.

10

Honor "La Famiglia"...
Respect Your Team Enough to Empower It

Growing up, the only teams we knew about were major league sports teams like the Phillies, the 76ers, the Flyers and 'da Birds (the Eagles). There was no talk of teams at the company where my father worked or among the employees at the local 5 & Dime. As kids we weren't involved in many teams. (Organized sports for kids didn't really exist back then…at least not in South Philly.) The Pomacs, our ragtag baseball team, was the only real sports team I ever played on. But looking back, there was a "team" right under my nose: my *family*.

I can almost see you rolling your eyes right now. I know it's cliché and trite to draw a comparison between a family and a team. But just indulge me for a moment. Why? Because for me, it's personal. For Italians, family is sacred.

La famiglia – my father, Al; me; my mother, Marion; my brother, Rich.

97

Italians are a family-based culture. Relationships are the cornerstone of the culture, and *la famiglia* (the family) is by far the most important one. I clearly remember my father saying in a very serious voice, "When you're out tonight, remember that you're representing our family. Don't do anything that would embarrass us." The cultural principle of family first is still evident today, even in Italian-Americans whose ancestors immigrated generations ago.

La famiglia exemplifies the principles of honor, respect and trust. In an Italian family, everyone has a role and contributes in some meaningful way, and everyone is clear about the common purpose. And while the nuclear family is the core of the team, the extended family plays a significant supporting role. In my family, if there was a project that needed to be done, there was never a question about who would help out – *everyone* did. Whether it was preparing holiday dinners or moving a household (it seemed someone was always getting married or upgrading to a 900-square-foot row house), it was a family/team affair.

I'll never forget the time we remodeled our house. Uncle Joe was the demolition expert – he tore down our kitchen wall practically with his bare hands. Dad assisted him, Mom cleaned up, Grandmom cooked, and my brother and I hauled off debris. When we took a family vacation (and with eight or nine people in the car, I do mean *family* vacation), everyone had a job to do: the men navigated and drove, the women searched for a motel and a grocery store to buy picnic supplies, and the kids…well, our job was mainly to leave each other alone and be quiet!

Merriam-Webster's Unabridged Dictionary defines *team* as "a group of specialists functioning as a collaborative unit." My family was a team in the true sense of the word. And as simplistic and idealistic as it may sound, I believe the family team of my youth can teach the business teams of today a few things.

Respect Your Team Enough to Empower It

Organizations throw millions of dollars a year at the issue of teamwork and team building. And yet I routinely receive calls from leaders who feel they're not getting the results they need from their teams, and at least 25 percent of the work I do with organizations involves helping teams work together and perform better. So what's going on?

I believe it's a lack of honor, respect and trust – the same core principles of la famiglia. In the business world, you can sum up these three concepts in one word: *empowerment*. Do organizations and their leaders honor, respect and trust their teams? In other words, do they truly *empower* their teams to successfully accomplish their stated goals and objectives? I think the answer is all too often, "No." Think about it…if a team isn't given the authority, the budget or the ability to achieve its purpose, I think it's fair to say the organization doesn't honor, respect or trust the team and its members.

If your team isn't producing the results you expect, I'm willing to bet a cheesesteak or two that it's because they don't feel empowered. (Whether they actually are empowered or not doesn't matter. As the adage goes, "Perception is reality.")

Let's be honest. We both know that many teams are teams in name only. Sometimes we create teams for the sake of appearances – because we need to show some kind of action in response to an exposed issue or concern. These teams often have no budget and no real authority to accomplish anything of significance.

Other times, we put together teams because we genuinely want solutions to organizational challenges…as long as those solutions fall within a tightly defined set of parameters, of course. These teams likely have a budget, but are frequently frustrated because they don't have the latitude to effect change. Management wants creativity and innovation, but the ideas better not be "too far out there." In other words, these teams are not empowered.

What's missing is a true voice, a valid contribution – both for the individuals and for the team as a whole. I see this scenario all too often. When I coach leaders and their teams, a recurring complaint I hear from *leaders* is that the individuals don't function together as a collaborative unit, let alone as a high performing team. Interestingly, the number one complaint I hear from *team members* is, "I'm on the team because my boss put me there, but I don't have a say in things. They expect me to work and to get results, but they don't really want my input." Is it any wonder these teams don't produce results?

I find that most leaders are well-intentioned and genuinely want to honor, respect and trust their teams, but don't know how to put those concepts into practice. They think that empowering their teams means letting them "do their own thing." But that often leads to an unfocused team. When teams aren't effective, it's often because individual members are not pulling in the same direction – usually because the direction wasn't clearly defined from the beginning. As a result, team synergy is diffused instead of concentrated on the project or purpose.

I recently worked with a team at a *progressive* company. The results of a survey had indicated that although the organization says it values professional development, employees didn't feel they had much opportunity for growth. So a task force was created, comprised of both management and non-management employees, to identify causes and make recommendations to address the issue. By the time I got involved, the team had already held two meetings, both of which had been frustrating. My first priority, as it is anytime I work with a team, was to determine whether or not this team was truly empowered to effect change. Let me share my observations, and you can draw your own conclusion.

Respect Your Team Enough to Empower It

When the task force was created, it was given no budget and no parameters for its work. Some team members arrived late or never showed up at all. I learned later than many felt the team was a waste of time. Individually, team members shared their concerns with me: concerns that the team's recommendations might ruffle some top-management feathers and that if the suggestions were seen as criticism, jobs would be in jeopardy; concerns that leadership would "laugh" at the team's proposed solutions or suggest that the team didn't understand the big picture; and concerns that "management won't listen to us…they're not going to let us make any real changes."

(It's interesting to note that I asked the team if anyone had ever been fired for being too vocal about senior management, and no one could remember such an incident. The point here is that team members' fears don't have to be rational to be real. Irrational fear is just as powerful as logical fear. Sometimes fears are founded; sometimes they're not. Either way, perception is reality.)

So what do you think? Was this an empowered team?

They may have looked the part to a casual observer, but in reality they weren't. Although I believe senior management had good intentions when it initiated this task force, it didn't give the team the tools it needed to accomplish its objectives. Nor did it remove obstacles and barriers (fears and concerns) that might hinder the team in its work. The bottom line? The company was wasting its time and money. Sadly, this example is not an isolated incident. Instead, it is painfully representative of many, many teams I come in contact with.

So what does it mean to honor, respect and trust your team… to empower them to fulfill their charter? It means giving them a true voice and meaningful involvement. It does not, however, necessarily mean giving them unilateral authority. Keep in mind that empowering a team with respect to one organizational issue doesn't translate to employee participation in all matters. Teams should operate just as families do, where some decisions are participative while others are mandated.

If we expect employees to be engaged team members who fulfill their responsibilities, we must fulfill our responsibilities as team leaders by:

- Providing clear, explicit objectives and parameters;
- Creating the genuine opportunity for teams and team members to win;
- Providing the budget and the resources to implement recommendations;
- Building an environment in which team members are not afraid to bring forth ideas that might be controversial or revolutionary;
- Actively listening to and acknowledging the inputs of the team;
- Accepting their recommendations whenever possible (and if not possible, providing timely, valid explanations as to why you can't).

For many years, GE used (and may still today) what it called a "tight-loose" philosophy with respect to setting parameters for its teams. On the "tight" side were the various parameters a team absolutely had to operate within, for example, a pre-determined budget, a specific timeframe, a market share requirement or a certain level of profitability. The "loose" side represented everything else a team could do to achieve results. In other words, as long as teams stayed within the established parameters, *how* they achieved the results was totally open. This tight-loose philosophy allows for a great deal of creativity, and I believe is one of the reasons GE has been so successful over the last 20 years.

Respect Your Team Enough to Empower It

Leading teams is tough. There's no question about it. It's even more difficult in flattened organizations and matrix-based organizations. The key is to truly empower your team and *then let them do their job*. If for whatever reason you can't genuinely empower them, then forgo the team and implement the changes yourself.

If you are a leader of leaders, help your leaders do their jobs more effectively by **modeling team leadership as well as teamwork with** other groups in your organization. In my South Philly neighborhood, there were at least five close-knit families that stood ready to help each other. Are you and your teams ready and willing to help each other and other departments?

My family was an unbeatable team: individuals were engaged and fully empowered to accomplish their responsibilities and the team functioned seamlessly because everyone was focused on the same goal. The culture of honor, respect and trust made for a truly rewarding experience. If you want unbeatable teams, authentically empower them– honor their role and their contribution, respect their input and trust their judgment.

How *You* Doin'?

- Is your work-group, department, division, or crew a true team or a team in name only? If yours is an in-name-only team, is it possible you could be contributing to the problem?

- Have you truly empowered your team(s)? Do you honor, respect and trust them to fulfill their charter?

- Does your team have the clarity it needs to fully participate and contribute?

StreetSavvy Techniques

By definition, if you're a leader, you lead a team. What can you do to ensure your team is an authentically empowered team?

1. **Select the right team members.** Organizations and leaders have a huge advantage over families: They can often choose who they want on their teams. You're probably familiar with the old saying, "You can't pick your family." Fortunately, you have the opportunity to pick the very best people to join your business "family."

   Choose people who have the skills, knowledge and background to deal with the issue at hand. Look for people who are candid and have the courage to speak their mind. Go for individuals who can demonstrate the attitude and aptitude for working on teams by asking them about specific team-based examples, accomplishments and results.

   According to team-effectiveness expert Donna Long, you should also consider individuals who are open to and value differences. She says, "A team that values diverse opinions and views has a foundation for greatness. They understand that potential conflict is not the kiss of death, but instead a healthy vehicle for checks and balances."

2. **Create a family atmosphere.** Start by encouraging team members to get to know one another. When people know each other on a social level, they're more likely to have empathy for each other's values, opinions and behaviors. This, in turn, leads to less bickering and a more focused team effort. For virtual teams with members in different locations, schedule social time during conference calls or try to plan face-to-face meetings if possible.

3. Clarify the team's purpose and parameters up front. A lack of clear purpose and straightforward guidelines is the biggest cause of team disempowerment and disengagement. Any time you put together a team, your first priority should be to clarify its purpose or to guide the group in defining the purpose.

Your second priority is to establish parameters. Effective parameters are "tight-loose" – tight enough that team recommendations are likely to be accepted and yet simultaneously broad enough for people to feel they have room to suggest meaningful and innovative ideas. Whether you're leading an ongoing team or a temporary task force can have a significant impact on parameters. For example, an ongoing team would likely operate under budgetary constraints, whereas a task force might be developing initiatives that then drive a budget to implement those initiatives. Each situation will be different, but consider the following areas when establishing parameters:

- Budget – e.g., "Your budget is $50,000, including implementation."
- People – e.g., "Maintain current staffing levels."
- Sales – e.g., "The plan must be implemented using existing sales resources."
- Return on investment – e.g., "Achieve 10 percent ROI by the second year."
- Operations – e.g., "New processes must be implemented within this fiscal year."
- Values – e.g., "Ensure that everything you do is in sync with organizational values."
- Branding – e.g., "Initiatives must support and enhance the brand."

4. **Perfect the team leader "balancing act."** An effective leader is actively involved, but not overly involved, with his or her team. I'll be honest…finding that balance is a very difficult thing to do. Give your team some autonomy. If you're in every meeting, chances are you'll dominate the conversation, stifle creativity and send the message that you don't trust your team. On the other hand, you need some "face time" with your team. Granted, meeting face-to-face with your team may not be easy if team members are in different offices or on different shifts, but it should be done whenever possible.

5. **Provide your team with candid feedback, coaching and recognition.** When your team provides you with updates, give them honest, constructive feedback. If they are outside of the parameters and headed down a rabbit trail, let them know sooner rather than later.

    Never forget that a team is made up of individuals who need personalized attention when it comes to communication, coaching and recognition. Don't make the mistake of thinking that "team" means you treat everyone the same. Are all team members paid the same or given the same amount of playing time on professional sports teams? Even in the flattest, most successful organizations, do all team members have the same responsibilities, authority, compensation or perks? The answer is "No" on both counts. Effective team leaders recognize and respond to the individual needs of each team member.

6. **Be an open conduit between your team and upper management.** A team can be very effective and produce great ideas, but if top management doesn't buy into them, it's all for naught. The leader who is politically savvy, understands what top management wants in terms of information and measurement, and has good presentation skills will serve his

team well. For example, if you know that *your* leader is heavily marketing-oriented, make sure your team regularly highlights the marketing benefits of their recommendations.

11

Live in the City of Brotherly Love...
Stop the Recognition Paradox

Philadelphia is one of the oldest cities, and perhaps the most historically significant, in the United States. During the 18th century, it was the center of independent thinking and politics that led to the American Revolution. The Declaration of Independence and the Constitution were drafted in Philadelphia and signed in Independence Hall. It was even our nation's capital for a period of time.

Founded in 1682 by William Penn, Philadelphia means "brotherly love" in Greek (from *philos* "loving" and *adelphos* "brother"). Penn's hope was that the city would be a model of its name and a shining example of freedom and religious tolerance.

Given that, it is interesting that Philadelphia has frequently had the dubious distinction of having one of the highest crime rates in the country. Over the years, the city has attracted national attention for government corruption, and like many other major cities, it's had a history of racial and ethnic conflict. Even the city's sports teams have a reputation for being excessively rough, and its fans are notoriously intolerant and unaccommodating of opposing teams and their fans. (Take my advice: unless you're up for some heavy duty verbal abuse, don't even think about wearing another team's jersey in the city, let alone at one of the sports complexes.) Although the story is often exaggerated, Eagles' fans once pelted a guy dressed as Santa Claus with snowballs.

As you might guess, many people see a paradox in what they perceive is an intolerant City of Brotherly Love. But many situations in life aren't what they appear to be. What seems to be virtuous or noble on the surface can be something else underneath. One such example is a business paradox that I am convinced is **the single most out-of-sync practice in organizations today: recognition.**

I am so tired of the platitudes about employees being an organization's most important asset. You find them on corporate web sites and in vision and value statements, executive speeches, annual reports, marketing materials and the press. And yet the cold, hard truth is that there is often no budget, minimal support, little time and virtually no accountability for caring for that asset. Of course, the human resources function exists to support and "care for" employees. That's not what I'm referring to. I'm talking about what happens directly on the front lines with employees on a daily basis. This is where the paradox exists: too many organizations and their leaders speak of the virtues of recognition but don't practice them.

Maybe the fact that we say that people are an "asset" is part of the problem. People are not property, machinery, pieces of equipment or items of value. They are human beings. I realize the intention behind this statement is positive, but I contend the reality is that employees are often treated like disposable assets rather than like human beings.

Another factor in this paradox is that the concept of recognition is misunderstood. *Recognition* is commonly defined as "appreciation for a person's or group's achievements." But showing appreciation means different things to different people. The concept of recognition varies greatly depending on age, gender, ethnicity and personal experience. To some it means money or tangible rewards. To others it's as simple as saying, "Thank you" or "Nice job."

Many leaders believe that recognition should only be given for exceptional achievements. I frequently encounter leaders who are not willing to express gratitude or pay a compliment to their employees. (Notice that I said they're "not willing" as opposed to "not able." I have very little patience with leaders who say they don't know *how* to give recognition. Gimme a break! Is it that hard to find something positive and compliment a person on it?) While it's true that recognition should be proportional to the performance, I think these leaders are missing the point. There are only so many babies to be saved from burning buildings. In other words, people can't do extraordinary things every day.

I know, I know…I hear you. Many of you are probably saying, "Al, if employees are just doing their jobs, why should I give them recognition?" How about because they're often doing their jobs in the face of crushing workloads, understaffed teams, tremendous pressures, limited resources, constant change and new technology. Let me ask you a few questions: Do you tell your spouse/partner, children, family members, maybe even friends, that you love them? How often? *Why* do you tell them?

People need to know that they are loved. Likewise, employees need to know that they are valued and appreciated. According to recognition expert Roz Jeffries, "One of the most significant needs of humankind is to feel valued, to feel important. Relationships end because one person doesn't feel appreciated. Teams break up because members don't feel valued. In the workplace, the need is no different. Employees feel valued when someone notices they've done a good job. A simple smile and 'thank you' are often all that is required."

If a team member adequately performs his or her job day after day, month after month, year after year, doesn't that person deserve some kind of acknowledgement? If not, it would be like never telling the important people in your life that you love them because they don't need to hear it.

What about you – don't *you* want recognition for doing your job? Or are you perfectly okay with your boss never acknowledging your work unless you do something exceptional? (By the way, some leaders tell me, "If I don't get recognition, I'm not going to give it." We have a word for that in Philly: *stupid*!)

Look, I'm not suggesting you give employees a standing ovation or a gold watch for doing their jobs. What I am suggesting is that you recognize their contributions and make certain they know you appreciate them. I'm suggesting you adopt a new definition of recognition, one that everyone should be able to agree on: treating people as worthwhile human beings.

If you think *I'm* disillusioned about recognition, you should hear what employees have to say about it! In the 35 years I've been in the corporate world, I can honestly say that I have never seen an employee survey that indicated leaders were giving enough recognition. Employee satisfaction with recognition typically ranges from 35 to 75 percent. Now you might think 75 percent satisfaction is pretty good. But that means in the best case scenario, a quarter of employees – one in four people – don't feel they're getting recognition.

Countless studies have proven that recognition enhances productivity, retention and customer service. So why don't more leaders utilize it? Perhaps it's because many leaders – at all levels – think recognition is a soft, touchy-feely HR issue, and not something for leaders out there in the trenches. It just sounds like something for the bleeding hearts, doesn't it? Others simply don't make it a high priority. Recognition is something they will get to sometime in the future – when they have more time, when sales pick up, when production improves, when this big project is over….

Even organizations that do believe in the importance of recognition and cascade it from top to bottom tolerate leaders who don't practice recognition. You know these kinds of leaders. They're the ones who say, "I'm not a recognition-kind-of-person. If employees just do their jobs and get results, we'll get along just fine." In a perfect world, organizations that truly value recognition would neither hire these leaders in the first place nor allow them to stay. But then again, it's not a perfect world.

Underlying leadership disbelief is the issue of measurement. It's extremely difficult, if not impossible, to measure the effects of providing recognition. Sure, you can measure productivity, retention and profit, but recognition isn't the only factor that affects those results. Consequently, you can't isolate the bottom-line impact of recognition. In the minds of many leaders, if you can't measure it, you shouldn't do it. And if you can't measure it, you shouldn't be held accountable for it. Right? Wrong!

Does your organization talk about the importance of recognition? Yes? Then it's on your accountability list, right? *Recognizing employees* is there alongside developing new markets, increasing sales, cutting costs, building customer relationships, boosting profits, increasing product/service quality and improving ROI? Oh, it's not? So recognition is really a "nudge and a wink" kind of thing?

No matter what anyone says, in most organizations financial results are the only measurements that really count. For all the talk about people being so important, when it comes right down to it, apparently they're not so important after all.

So where does that leave you? I'll tell you where…in charge! You can take control and provide recognition within your team or department. You don't need higher-level approval to treat employees with respect and acknowledge their work. Just do it!

Might it require some courage? Yes. Especially if your boss thinks recognition is for bleeding hearts or gives you the wink that says, "Just get the results. Don't worry about that recognition stuff." You must have the courage to say, "As long as I get the results, I should have some flexibility with *how* I get them." Why would you stick your neck out like that? Because **recognition works**, and it's in everyone's best interest…even your boss's!

So…recognition is easy to do, increases employee engagement and retention, leads to better customer service and enhances the employer brand…sounds like an exceptional YROI. If you're still not convinced, consider these returns on your recognition investment:

> ➤ **Improved productivity**. What oil does for a piece of equipment, recognition does for people – it helps them work smoother, work better, work longer. Results of a study by the Council on Communication confirm that **recognition for a job well done is the top motivator of employee performance**.

> ➤ **Better results**. Team members who are recognized give discretionary effort that directly impacts the bottom line. Let's be honest – you don't give recognition just to be a nice person, although it wouldn't hurt. You do it to get results. I'm sure even Attila the Hun gave recognition to his men. I can hear him now…"Good pillage! Many

suffered!" Perhaps that's why he was so "successful." What gets recognized gets repeated!

Have I busted your chops enough yet? I'm just trying to make a point, albeit a very important point. But I'll let you in on a little secret: I teach this stuff, and occasionally I still forget to give recognition. It's not about being perfect. It's about continuous improvement – being better today than you were yesterday.

Let me tell you a quick story: Until just a few years ago, many parts of Philadelphia were overrun with panhandlers and homeless people. But the City of Brotherly Love, perhaps more than any other city in the United States, has solved its problem with chronic homelessness. The city figured out that to truly help its homeless people, it had to get them into permanent housing and provide them with immediate counseling services.

The leader of this movement is a nun, Sister Mary Scullion. She has spent the last 20-plus years walking the streets of Philadelphia, encouraging the homeless and mentally ill to "come inside" and get help. She's trained outreach teams and built (or persisted until local government built) hundreds of housing units. In Philadelphia, she's known as "the Mother Teresa of the homeless." It's estimated that in the mid-1990s, there were 4,500 homeless people living in Philadelphia, and half of those were on the street at any given time. Ten years later, there were approximately 130 homeless people. One woman has almost single-handedly dismantled the paradox of the City of Brotherly Love.

It only takes one person to dismantle the recognition paradox within an organization…to deliver tangible results while treating people as worthwhile human beings. *Could that person be you?*

How *You* Doin'?

- Do you believe recognition is an essential factor in achieving organizational results?

- In your organization, are leaders' actions in sync with what the organization says about recognition?

- Do you look for opportunities to give recognition, or do you wait for people to do something spectacular?

- Are you willing to give recognition to your team even if your leader doesn't think it's important?

StreetSavvy Techniques

1. **Get in sync.** If you – as an individual leader or as an organization – aren't going to give recognition, *then stop talking about it!* At least your employees won't expect it.

2. **Develop self-awareness.** You can't get better at giving recognition until you know where you're starting from. If your organization doesn't use 360° assessments, you'll have to ask your team how well you recognize them. Encourage them to be candid and remember to clarify your definition of recognition – treating people as worthwhile human beings. Otherwise, you may not get valid feedback.

   Another approach is to ask your team to indicate anonymously on paper the number of positive and negative interactions they have with you on a daily basis. According to Lee Colan, Ph.D., author of *7 Moments…That Define Excellent Leaders*, research by the former chairman of Gallup, Donald Clifton, revealed that workgroups with at least a 3:1 ratio of positive to negative interactions with their leader were significantly more productive than those having less than a 3:1 ratio. In other words, productive teams had at least three positive interactions for every one negative interaction. What do you suppose the ratio is for your team…3:1? 1:1? Or could it be 1:3? Wouldn't it be interesting to find out?

Oh, one more thing: If your employees act uneasy or uncomfortable when you ask them for feedback on how well you give recognition, that's a sure sign you need some improvement!

3. Just do it. Recognition isn't rocket science. It's relatively easy to implement. Roz Jeffries suggests, "Think of yourself as a gardener, with a watering can in one hand and a can of fertilizer in the other. Occasionally, you have to pull some weeds. But most of the time, you just nurture and tend and watch your employees grow."

4. Multitask. Giving recognition is one of the few situations in which multitasking is actually effective. Remember that recognition is not a new, extra task to be added to your plate. It should be a part of the things you're already doing. Or put another way, recognition should be an integral part of the way you do the things you do.

For example, developing employees by offering them high-profile projects is an effective way to achieve results and provide recognition at the same time. Or let's assume that you're giving a tour to someone from outside your department. As you approach the area where an employee (we'll call him Charlie) is working, instead of talking about Charlie in the third person, introduce him to your visitor. Ask Charlie to explain to the visitor what he and his teammates do. It doesn't take any more time, yet it shows that you think Charlie is worthwhile. Would you consider that recognition? I bet Charlie would!

12

Scrub Your Steps...
Polish Your Organizational Pride

There was a time in South Philadelphia in the 1950s when a visitor would have thought that everyone worked for the city. Residents picked up trash in the streets, shoveled snow and put salt down on slippery sidewalks. The care and maintenance of common areas was everyone's responsibility...and there were no homeowners' association dues. People had pride in their homes, pride in their neighborhoods and pride in their city. No self-respecting person would allow his or her property to reflect poorly on the family. And nowhere was that more evident than in the meticulous care given to the front steps of people's homes.

White marble steps on Hutchison Street in South Philly.

The steps (not stoops – those are found in New York) that led up to just about every house I can remember in South Philly were made of white marble. People (usually the women) didn't just sweep their steps, they scrubbed them…on their hands and knees, with water, Ajax cleanser and a stiff, heavy bristled brush. And because they were concerned that someone might "break their neck," the steps were always dried with a rag. Even the railings were wiped down.

How often do you suppose the people of South Philly scrubbed their steps? Once or twice a year? Every few months? Gimme a break! How about once or twice a week! No joke – I'm completely serious! I can even remember a few fanatics in the neighborhood who scrubbed their steps every other day to keep them white. Was it pride run amuck? I don't think so.

Most of the adults in our neighborhood were first-generation descendants of Italian immigrants who had come to America and struggled to establish roots in a new country. And because of the courage and fortitude of their parents, these people were able to achieve a piece of the American Dream: home ownership, something their parents for the most part hadn't achieved. It was as if those white marble steps, scrubbed and polished, represented everything they and their ancestors had achieved. I call it pride hard earned and well deserved.

This tremendous sense of pride carried over to the workplace, too. It was a privilege to have a good job with a good company. Employees took pride in producing and delivering a quality product or service. Employees were committed to the company, and the company was equally committed to employees.

Now, fast-forward 50 years to the New Millennium. I don't know about you, but I don't see much pride in Corporate America. Which do you hear more frequently – people promoting or criticizing their organizations? How often do you see employees wearing or using corporate-identity pieces (hats, shirts, cups, etc.) *outside* of work? When you first meet new people and ask about their professional lives, do they tell you what company they work for or only what they do? Do you sense that they are enthusiastic about the organization they work for? For that matter, can others tell whether *you* are proud of the organization you work for?

Organizational pride may not be dead, but it certainly appears to be on life support.

What has happened over the last five decades to crush organizational pride? Plenty! For one thing, corporate corruption and unethical behavior are far more commonly known today. Notice I didn't say "more common," but "more commonly *known*." Corporate corruption has been around since the days of ancient Rome, but organizations were better able to keep it under wraps and out of the public eye until recently.

It's easy to see how employees – and leaders – of organizations that have been caught in dishonest, unethical or illegal situations would not have warm and fuzzy feelings about their employers. But this distrust and lack of pride has spread like a virus to employees of honest, law-abiding organizations. Although there truly are few unethical companies relative to the total number of organizations, the unspoken feeling is, "If some are guilty, all must be guilty."

Another reason for the current lack of organizational pride is cynicism. A Gallup survey of 700,000 employees revealed that 60 to 80 percent of employees either were not engaged or were actively disengaged. The survey also found that the majority of these employees were cynical about their organizations and that the longer employees were with a company, the less engaged and more cynical they became. I'm pretty sure you can't be cynical and proud at the same time. It stands to reason that if cynicism increases over time, there will be a corresponding decrease in organizational pride.

This high level of cynicism among employees is due in part to the fact that Corporate America, led by Wall Street, has succumbed to the delusion that CEOs are the primary drivers of profits and results. CEOs, before you get your noses out of joint, let me say that clearly you play a critical role. But as far as I can tell, a healthy bottom line will *always* come down to individual employees and leaders doing their jobs effectively, day in and day out. No matter how brilliant a CEO is, he/she can't make a dime of profit without the efforts of the workforce.

It's hurtful, to say the least, for employees to work hard for the company and then go without raises and bonuses or to see their friends and co-workers laid off while the CEO gets a bigger compensation package (including salary, bonus and stock options). In this type of business climate, it's surprising to me that there aren't even *more* employees who are cynical about their organizations.

Front-line leaders typically cannot change the causes of diminished pride, but they can help create a positive culture that is the precursor to organizational pride. Pride usually isn't a *have-to* in organizations, but it certainly ought to be a *want-to*. Unfortunately, many leaders think organizational pride is old fashioned and immaterial in today's technology-driven, fast-paced global economy. (Come on, admit it. When you saw the title of this chapter, you almost skipped it because you didn't think it was relevant, right?) That old-fashioned status, plus an emphasis on measurable results (and the fact that organizational pride is difficult to measure), means leaders perceive there is little return on investment for focusing on or encouraging organizational pride.

But common sense, along with studies by Towers Perrin, The Hay Group and Deloitte, indicate that pride in one's organization leads to employee engagement. Engagement leads to productivity, which in turn leads to increased profits. Not coincidentally, pride absolutely matters at the "Most Admired" and most successful organizations. Yahoo, SAS, Caterpillar, FedEx, W.L. Gore and Con-Way Transportation – all of these organizations make *internal* branding and organizational pride a top priority.

Caterpillar Logistics Services provides world-class supply chain solutions and services, and executives come from all over the world to benchmark them. Entering their warehouse is like walking into a hospital it is so clean and organized. Warehouse tours are typically given by employees, and visitors can easily sense their pride in the way they talk about their people, their culture, even their equipment. And wouldn't you be proud knowing that people fly halfway around the world to see how you do your work?

At one time on its corporate website, Yahoo! described itself this way: "Yahoo! is the premier Internet media conglomerate. The smoking hot guide to everything Web. And the most essential Internet service for consumers and businesses ever known to mankind. Despite our overly giddy enthusiasm, these descriptions are not far off the mark. Yahoos are, in fact, helping define the future of the Internet." Yahoos? They've even named themselves. Sounds like organizational pride run amuck…in a good way! It's too bad so many other organizations can't say the same thing.

Now, if thousands of tech-savvy Yahoos think organizational pride isn't old fashioned, do you think perhaps you should reconsider your position on it?

I'm not suggesting a return to a simplistic, "good-old-days" approach to organizational pride. We need a different spin on organizational pride – one that's in sync with the modern workplace, younger employees and the realities of a technology-based global economy. Today's employees can't depend on a company, a job or even a consistent set of responsibilities. But they can depend on, and find pride in, an organizational culture that values and acknowledges them and their efforts.

To this day, I respond to the question about where I'm from with pride: "South Philly!" The people who lived there had pride in themselves, in their accomplishments and in their neighborhood. Those gleaming white marble steps were a tangible representation of that pride. Would you like your employees to have that same level of pride in your organization? Think about how valuable that would be when the inevitable business challenges and negatives pop up, which they most certainly will. That's when you'll discover just how powerful organizational pride can be.

How *You* Doin'?

➢ Do you model organizational pride both at work and outside of work?

➢ Do you recognize and encourage team members who exhibit a high level of pride?

➢ When you hire or promote people, do you consider past demonstrations of organizational pride as one of the criteria?

StreetSavvy Techniques

1. Determine the level of organizational pride that exists – or doesn't exist – within your team or department. You can tell a lot about the level of pride in an organization or team through simple observation. How do employees treat each other? Are the physical surroundings well cared for? How are customers (including internal customers) treated?

Here's another quick and easy way to evaluate organizational pride: Ask yourself what percentage of your employees would wear a hat or shirt with your company name on it? How many would buy something with your corporate logo? If asked what they do for a living, would your employees respond with their job title alone, or would they also mention your company's name? The answers to these questions will give you a general idea of your team's level of pride.

2. **Take advantage of your influence as a leader to enhance organizational pride.** You have a unique opportunity to reinforce the positive aspects of your organization with your team. Remind employees about the good works your company does in the community, awards your organization has received, positive media, etc. When leaders genuinely model organizational pride, without brown-nosing or being schmaltzy, eventually it rubs off on employees.

3. **Be very cognizant of your potential negative effect on organizational pride.** When an organization does something that is perceived as unfair, inappropriate or unrealistic, leaders are put in a very difficult position. If you badmouth the organization or senior leadership, it sends the message to employees that it's okay for them to do the same. Furthermore, it makes you look bad…and not just because speaking critically of senior leadership isn't appropriate. Statements like, "What were they thinking when they…" indicate to your team that not only do you disagree, but also that you weren't able to do anything about the situation. After just a few instances like this, employees will get the message loud and clear that you don't have any influence in the organization.

Although it may be tempting to criticize organizational decisions – especially the ones that truly are poor decisions –

resist the urge. The reality is that you accomplish nothing, other than damaging organizational pride, by feeding the fire. Instead, I recommend you do the following:

- Ferret out the reasons and rationale behind the organization's action or decision. For example, if the company spent a lot of money to redo the front of the building not long after a workforce reduction, you may discover that the city passed a new ordinance that required the work to be done. You may not always agree with the logic behind a senior management decision, but at least you'll know the reasons.

- If at all possible, share this information with your team. You're much better off giving them the honest reasons behind a decision or policy than letting their imaginations run wild about what went on behind closed doors. When employees understand that changes were in fact thought out by management, even if they disagree with the reasons, it can actually enhance organizational pride.

- Focus employees' attention on the positive aspects of the change. There is almost always a silver lining to any decision or policy change. Find it and promote it!

- And finally, if employees ask you point-blank what you think about a management decision that you don't agree with, instead of criticizing, simply say something like, "Please respect the fact that this situation puts me in a difficult position, and I'd rather not comment." They may draw the conclusion that you disagree, but you've maintained your integrity as a leader.

13

Play Halfball and Dead Box...
Get Creative and Have Some Fun

If nothing else, South Philly kids were inventive.

We learned to be creative and make our own fun with what little we had. Rolled newspaper tied with string served as a football. A sawed-off broom handle made a respectable bat. With only a ten-cent pimple ball and a few items you could find lying around, you could play an almost endless number of games: Slapball, Wallball, Boxball, Stickball, Stepball, etc. (Notice a common theme?)

We could even have fun with things other people considered trash. Case in point: "dead" pimple balls. Over time, pimple balls would crack or split from being exposed to the elements or run over by a car. That's when our creativity would take over, and we'd cut the balls in half for Halfball. (Apparently our creativity didn't extend to the names we gave our games!) Then it was off to the "ballpark" – the south wall of Francis Scott Key Elementary School.

To play Halfball, the pitcher stood with his back to the wall and threw underhand "mooners" with the face of the Halfball toward the batter. The batter, who always pretended to be a Phillies player like Richie Ashburn, then hit the Halfball against the wall. If someone caught the ball as it bounced off the wall, the batter was out. When the ball wasn't caught, the batter was awarded bases according to where the ball hit on the wall – the higher on the wall, the better the hit. So, a ball hit to the top of the first story was a single. Over "the spaghetti" (our nickname for the decorative trim that separated the stories) was a double, over the second-story spaghetti a triple, and over the third-floor spaghetti…a home run! Halfball was so fun it became more popular than any of the other ball games.

A game of Halfball in the streets.

Beeries – bottle caps from beer or soda bottles – were another castoff item that offered lots of possibilities. Although we usually dug them out of the trash or picked them up off the street, we were always on the lookout for pristine beeries that could be found near soda machines or in the iced tubs at the drug store. Unlike the bottle caps of today, beeries had cork on the inside. If we were careful, we could pop that cork out in one piece using a knife. Then we'd put the cap on the outside of a shirt, put the cork on the inside and snap them back together. Instant button! Beeries also made great accessories for homemade scooters. (Picture an orange crate, pieces of wood and metal roller-skate wheels.)

But by far the best use of beeries was for playing Dead Box. To play this common street game, we'd use chalk "borrowed" from school to draw a large square "game board" on a smooth part of the street. Players attempted to flick their beeries into each numbered box, in order from 1 through 12. After reaching the last box, the player would shoot for the box with the skull, called "the dead box." Once a player made it to the dead box, he became "poison," and any beery he hit was dead and out of the game. The last person "alive" was the winner.

That's it. Nothing expensive or elaborate. But man, did we have some fun! We spent hours and hours playing Halfball and Dead Box, and it was the most fun I can remember having between the ages of 9 and 16. Playing street games provided balance for my schoolwork and household chores, my "jobs" at the time.

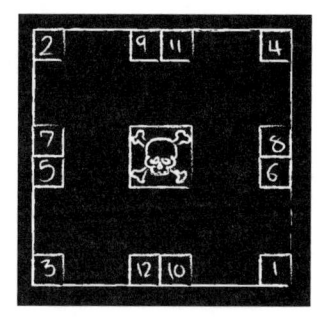

Layout of a chalk Dead Box.

Today, there is a call for more fun in the workplace, especially from the younger generations. But they're not the only ones who think a little fun and frivolity are a good thing. Most productivity and motivational experts agree that **the more people enjoy themselves at work, the more productive they are**. Even psychologists report that we need more joy and stress-relieving entertainment in our lives.

Progressive organizations no longer see workplace fun as inappropriate or in conflict with positive results. In fact, many of today's most successful companies not only believe that fun is crucial to their bottom-line success, but they also know *how* to have fun. Organizations like Southwest Airlines, Starbucks and the Container Store consciously and intentionally dedicate time, money and resources to having fun.

There's a reason why Southwest Airlines is one of the most-often benchmarked companies. It is the most consistently profitable airline in the industry and often posts a profit even when other carriers are struggling with economic downturns and high fuel prices. Fun in the workplace has been a key organizational value since the company's inception. If a company with such consistently impressive bottom-line results thinks having fun is important, perhaps there's something to it!

Southwest's culture of fun is profound in yet another respect. Most people would consider having hundreds of passengers' lives in your hands (as do pilots, flight attendants, mechanics, etc.) to be a very serious job, and I'd agree. Can you work at a serious job and have fun at the same time? Safety guru and workplace-fun expert Richard Hawk says, "If a team's purpose involves a serious matter, it's all the more reason why having fun should be a main concern. **People (and teams) who have fun perform better, get along better and make fewer mistakes**. Realize this: *fun* and *play* don't mean the same thing. To have fun doing something means to enjoy the process; to play means to engage in an activity strictly for enjoyment."

If done well, fun at work can produce double returns – fun for fun's sake plus business results such as team building, professional development and even meaningful culture change. For example, a financial services client held an executive retreat in San Diego to develop their strategic plan for the coming year. As part of the event, I took all 45 attendees to the San Diego Zoo and split them into teams. Each team had to select an animal and connect something about that animal to the issues being discussed at the meeting. The next day each team gave a brief presentation. Some used pictures they'd taken at the zoo; some did skits; others acted out animal behaviors. A few of my personal favorites were:

- ➢ comparing elephant behavior to slow decision-making;
- ➢ acting out monkey behaviors to illustrate the dangers of lack of focus;
- ➢ using a giraffe to demonstrate the need to look far ahead and to be "head and shoulders" above the competition.

Top leadership was amazed at the out-of-the-box thinking their people displayed when given the opportunity. This was a fun activity that added only slightly to the overall cost of the conference but had a huge effect on the success of the meeting. The organization, which had a conservative culture, discovered that fun and productive results are not mutually exclusive. In fact, they can be directly connected.

If fun enhances productivity and performance, why don't more organizations encourage fun in the workplace?

I think many leaders fear that fun will distract employees from their job responsibilities and that fun activities might get out of control or become inappropriate. But when you have a solid foundation of accountability, you don't have to worry about employees goofing off too much or fun getting out of hand. A culture of fun goes hand in hand with a culture of accountability. (See Chapters 1 and 20 for more on accountability.) Members of the organization understand performance expectations, respect the cultural values and behave accordingly. For proof of this, consider again Southwest Airlines. This organization is *the* benchmark for fun in the workplace, and yet it must operate in accordance with complex FAA regulations and be responsible for thousands of people's lives every day.

Perhaps the lack of fun in the workplace is an issue of cost. Maybe organizations and their leaders think budgets are too tight to spend money on fun. Gimme a break! If a bunch of kids have the ingenuity to have a great time with a "worthless" ball, a broom handle and some bottle caps, surely organizations can have some fun even with little or no budget. I think it's more an issue of creativity than cost.

I know for a fact that you can create a culture of fun despite the pressures of daily business life. For a number of years I was a co-owner of a human resources training and development company. Many of our employees said it was the best place they'd ever worked. Over the years, our leaders and employees organized events such as a paintball war, a golf tournament and a murder-mystery dinner party.

But what really made our company different was that we made fun a regular occurrence…and it cost us virtually nothing. Almost everyone in the office had some kind of fun nickname. On birthdays and employment anniversaries, we wrote funny poems or "roasted" the individual. Our in-house graphics guru superimposed co-workers' faces on pictures of comic book heroes and frequently created and gave goofy awards to colleagues. If someone dared to take their shoes off, a shoe thief "stole" the shoes, and the barefoot person had to hunt them down. The president had a habit of grabbing employees for a quick game of Pass the Pigs in the lunchroom. We hung a large brass bell in a central location and rang it every time we made a big sale. People would come out of their offices and gather in the hall to hear the good news and share in the excitement.

You'd be surprised what you can do with a little imagination and ingenuity. At one Christmas party, the owners – including yours truly – did a chin play. (In a chin play, the "actors" are upside down. Eyes and a nose are drawn on each actor's chin, and the result is a chin "person." Yes, it's odd, but it's hilarious.) For our annual users' conference, one leader made a rap video to introduce her department to our clients. Each member of her team, from 20-something males to a woman in her 50s, dressed up in "street" clothes and rapped their name, role within the company and how they served customers. It was hilarious and a huge hit with our clients.

The leaders of our organization intentionally created a culture of fun. There was a pervasive feeling that it was okay – even important – to goof around, blow off some steam and have some fun. As a result, we had extremely dedicated and loyal employees who consistently gave above-and-beyond discretionary effort. Many employees worked at the company for 8, 10, 15 years. Not long ago, I went to a party for the 50ish woman in the rap video. She's been with the company for more than 20 years. At our little company, we learned what companies like Southwest Airlines have always known – that fun positively affects the bottom line.

Fun in the workplace comes down to you, the leader. You are the single biggest factor in your team's culture (and as a leadership group, the single biggest factor in your organization's culture). You set the tone, the mood and the atmosphere of your workplace. Start now. Don't put off having fun until you can pull off a big elaborate shindig. If you do, it will never happen. Start small and build over time.

The need we have as children to have fun and "just be kids" never really leaves us. We simply push it out of our minds. But just as a kid who goes out to play will be more settled and focused when it comes time to do homework, adults who have some good-natured fun on a regular basis will be more productive, more creative and more focused when it comes to their work.

Most employees are looking for reasons to *stay* with your organization, so why not give them one? Have some fun. Even though at times I complained about my South Philly neighborhood, I never wanted to move to a big house in the suburbs…they didn't play Halfball or Dead Box there.

How *You* Doin'?

➤ Does your organization value fun in the workplace? Do *you* value fun within the culture of your team or department?

➤ Do you recognize others who have fun, or do you think of them as goof-offs?

➤ Do you have fun at work, and do you model appropriate fun-loving behaviors?

StreetSavvy Techniques

1. Keep fun "stuff" around the office. Gather a supply of inexpensive games and toys that people can play for a quick break. There are a wide variety of electronic handheld games available: Yahtzee, Poker, Deal or No Deal, Sudoku, Rummy, Hangman, Battleship, etc. Also consider puzzles, challenge games like Rubik's Cubes, and toys such as Etch-A-Sketches, miniature remote control cars and Hacky Sacks. Games that more than one person can play in 10 minutes or less, like Pass the Pigs, are great to keep in the break room.

Tired, stressed or frazzled employees who take a brief "fun break" will go back to their work reenergized and refreshed. Many companies report that these fun breaks are the very times when employees develop innovative ideas or solve complex problems. And remember, if you've built a culture of accountability, you have no reason to worry about people having too much fun.

2. Enlist senior executives and upper management in modeling playful behaviors (and make sure you do the same). Leadership must demonstrate through their *actions* that fun is part of your culture, that fun in the workplace is encouraged and that having fun at work really is okay. Remember, people are watching. It doesn't matter what you say or your organizational values state – if leadership isn't having fun, no one else will either. When the senior vice president of finance does his Elvis impersonation at the next meeting, your employees will know you're serious about having fun.

3. **Get employees involved**. Fun in the workplace is the perfect opportunity for employee involvement and participation. Find fun-loving, enthusiastic employees and designate them as your Ambassadors of Fun (after asking them, of course). Look for people who always seem to have a smile on their face and have a knack for making a lot of fun out of nothing (think Halfball).

Give your Ambassadors the responsibility and the *authority* to encourage creativity and fun in the workplace. (Oh yeah, and a small budget wouldn't hurt either!) Let them decide if they want another family picnic or would rather rent out a laser tag or whirlyball arena for the day. Employee-driven fun helps to ensure that your fun doesn't get stale. The surest way to turn something from fun to boring is to do it over and over again. Skip the traditional holiday party this year and go play Halfball instead!

14

"Roof It"... Select the Top Priorities and Get Rid of the Rest

When I visit South Philly these days, I find myself asking, "When did the neighborhood get so small?" As a kid, I never realized what close quarters we lived and played in. Perhaps that was because I was small then. It's all a matter of perspective, I guess. But the reality of growing up in South Philadelphia was a reality of small spaces – a small house with small rooms; a small kitchen and a small pantry; small streets to drive, park and play on; a small grocery store on the corner; and in some ways, small minds (see Chapter 18 about provincialism!)

Here's something else interesting: growing up, we never knew we were financially challenged because our parents were too proud and too guarded with that type of information to ever let us know it. We always considered ourselves middle class, but in retrospect, we were probably lower middle-class at best.

At the same time, we clearly understood that it was unacceptable to waste things – especially food – and my parents didn't spend a lot of money on eating out, fancy vacations or upscale clothing. And you know what? I never missed any of those things. I feel like I had a great childhood.

I will say, however, that all these space and financial limitations meant we had to be efficient and organized. We kept only the essentials, learned to prioritize carefully and were judicious with our spending. Hmm…that seems similar to the mantra of business executives who constantly push for "leaner and meaner" organizations. My mother was the original CFO. She bought only what we needed at the moment and nothing else. And with every meal came the same admonishment: "Only put on your plate what you're going to eat…and you'd better finish it all!" Sounds to me like just-in-time inventory and "minimize waste."

Perhaps you think that growing up under these circumstances was depressing or difficult. Actually, it was just the opposite – it was easy. What to wear? There were very few choices…only a couple pair of jeans and a few shirts. What to eat? We had only the grocery store, butcher shop and street vendors to pick from. Where to go? You could go only as far as your legs could carry you. Fewer choices meant greater "productivity" and "efficiency," and it taught me to focus on the essentials – a lesson that has served me well throughout my life.

Most people in today's business world face the opposite challenge: they have too many choices – too much work, too many "top priorities." There's more to do than can possibly be done in a reasonable amount of time. An article in *Fast Company* magazine entitled "Don't Manage Time, Manage Yourself" by David Beardsley states that the average businessperson has a chronic backlog of 200 to 300 hours of uncompleted work. That's five to seven *weeks* worth of work! How is a person to catch up?

You can't.

In addition, in today's "flatter" organizations, employees and leaders often have conflicting priorities because they serve multiple internal customers and have "dotted-line" accountability to various positions. These people are faced almost daily with the question, "Whose project am I going to do first? Who am I going to keep happy and who am I going to tick off?"

Organizations and leaders expect a great deal from employees, but often don't do a good enough job of helping them understand the priorities. Which, if you think about it, is a bit ironic. Organizations want to increase profits by producing more with fewer employees, yet inadvertently make it more difficult on employees to increase productivity and achieve better results by not clearly identifying priorities.

Combined, these factors create a tremendous amount of stress. When you constantly feel like you can't get it all done, coupled with being uncertain about what to focus on first, it's extremely hard to stay energized and engaged. Stress and safety expert Richard Hawk tells us that chronic stress:

- Impairs focus and attention to detail;
- Reduces productivity;
- Increases disengagement;
- Diminishes quality of work and quality of work life;
- Is one of the leading causes of absenteeism;
- Increases medical claims and insurance costs;
- Is quickly becoming one of the top causes of worker compensation cases.

Something has to give. People need help determining which of the myriad of projects, tasks, deadlines and meetings they're juggling are most important. "Why do they need help?" you may ask. "Can't they figure it out on their own?"

We can't expect employees to effectively prioritize if we don't give them the necessary information. In many cases, employees don't have access to the organization's strategic priorities. As a result, they don't see the big picture or understand how their work ties to the organization's key objectives. The funny thing about priorities is that every organization and every team has them (or better have them), and yet frequently, they're not clear to the very individuals who have to carry them out on a daily basis. I recently heard an executive say, "Everything is a priority"…everything except common sense on his part apparently!

One of your roles as a leader is to help set and promote realistic expectations with respect to workload and priorities for your team members. As with so many other issues, you are the middleman – the connection between senior management and your team. Use your knowledge of the organization's strategic plan to help employees better prioritize their responsibilities.

Author Scott Friedman shares this insight from Jeffrey Miller, President and CEO of Documentum: "There is always too much work to do and not enough time to do it. In order to prevent insanity, frustration and burnout, we need to develop our own pace and then develop laser-like focus on our priorities."

I agree with Jeffrey, and at the same time, I don't think he goes far enough. Let me tell you the truth that no one else is likely to tell you: simply reprioritizing is never going to solve the problem. If you want to quickly and permanently increase productivity, you're going to have to *eliminate* some so-called priorities for your team.

That's right – you read it right. I said **eliminate**.

As long as you and your team continue to have the same number of tasks, activities and projects on your plate, some things will probably never get done. To prove my point, let me ask you: As a leader, you probably do an effective job of prioritizing, right? How many items are still on your to-do list from last week, last month, *last year*?

Select the Top Priorities and Get Rid of the Rest

That's what I thought.

If the reality is that you're not going to get to all of them, then why not get rid of them? You have to ask yourself, if something has been on your to-do list or your team's priority list for more than a few months and it's still not done, is it really that important? Apparently you're operating just fine without the benefits of completing it. Even if it's a low priority, keeping it on the list day after day after day gives you "agida" (Italian for heartburn) and creates unnecessary pressure for your team.

I also contend that there are likely activities and tasks your team members are doing on a regular basis that are virtually worthless in terms of return. These are often processes that were valuable at one time but are now outdated, meetings that have become unproductive, or reports and analyses are no longer worth the return on the time invested in them.

Perhaps you're skeptical and think there are no tasks or activities you or your team could eliminate. Let me give you some real-world examples. I know of a company that negotiates literally hundreds of healthcare contracts each year. Their process requires that each potential supplier's annual report be included with the proposed contract. Insiders tell me that no one ever looks at these reports. Now consider that over the course of a year, different people within the company may write as many as 10 contracts with one supplier in 10 different product categories. This means that someone must locate, download and archive the exact same reports, 10 times a year. Multiply that by hundreds of contracts a year and you start to see how much unnecessary work is literally being repeated over and over again. Imagine the time that's being wasted that could be spent on tasks that actually drive results!

Apparently, some inside the company have suggested that they create a central "library" where each supplier's information is kept (and updated once a year) for those who want to review it. But making this kind of a change hasn't been "high on the priority list."

Negotiators in this company spend a tremendous amount of time handling contracts they are 99.99 percent certain will never be awarded, but still have to be negotiated because the supplier responded to a request for proposal. (This requirement is part of the organization's process because they negotiate contracts on behalf of other healthcare companies.) It's a "reality" of their business that wastes not just the negotiators' time, but also the resources of analysts and the legal department. Imagine the productivity that could take place if this organization had the courage to go to its customers and develop a better process.

To be fair, I want to point out that this organization has recently made a change to its procedures that represent a big step in the right direction. Executive committees used to approve all contracts whether they were for $100 million or $1 million, rendering these teams far less productive than they could be. (For more on working with teams, see Chapter 10.) Now, contracts under a certain dollar threshold are awarded by lower level committees. The result? Productivity has increased, while the amount of time it takes to get contracts awarded has been reduced.

These are examples from just one organization. I know there are similar situations in your organization too. They exist in virtually every company I've ever dealt with.

When I was a kid in Philly, we used the term "roof it," which meant to lose or get rid of something (forever, in our minds). The neighborhoods were tightly packed with two-story row houses, each with a flat roof. We often accidentally hit balls onto the roofs during Stickball or Halfball games. Of course, once a ball was "roofed," it was gone and the game was over.

SELECT THE TOP PRIORITIES AND GET RID OF THE REST

Row houses with flat roofs on Hutchison Street in South Philly where I grew up. I wonder how many items have been "roofed" here over the years...

Over time, the roofs of South Philly become a repository for other things we wanted to get rid of. I remember the time I was dating a girl and gave her a ring. When she broke up with me, she gave me the ring back. I was so angry and upset that I roofed the ring – I literally threw it on top of our house. As odd as it may sound, it provided me with a certain sense of closure, and I was able to move on. Years later, a buddy reminded me of that and said, "When you roofed that ring, it was like putting her into oblivion. She was gone."

I'm calling on leaders at all levels to take a stand, identify top priorities and have the courage to stop unproductive, wasteful activities. In other words, ***select the best and roof the rest!*** Create a more narrow, focused world for your team by helping them zero-in on key priorities and eliminate non-ROI activities. Practice what I call "zero-based prioritizing," a concept that's similar to zero-based budgeting. Periodically (once a year, once a quarter – whatever time period works best for your situation), rethink which projects, activities, tasks and initiatives are truly important in terms of producing results. Ask the very tough question of yourself and of your team, "Are there some things we're doing that we don't have to do or that we can do more efficiently?" Then focus on the high-impact activities and either eliminate or outsource the others.

Will you be able to completely do away with all unproductive tasks? No. It's a lot like turnover. You'll never be able to eradicate it, but you can certainly improve it dramatically. When you select the best and roof the rest, **every task you eliminate frees up precious time and resources for you and your team to apply toward those activities that directly drive results and profit.** Keeping people sane, unstressed and productive will give you the biggest bang for your buck.

How *You* Doin'?

- Can you definitively answer the question, "What are my priorities?"

- Can each of your employees definitively answer the question, "What are my priorities?"

- Do your team members understand the big picture and how their work connects to it?

- When you give team members new tasks and projects, do you just pile more on their plate, or do you help them eliminate some existing activities to make room for the new ones?

StreetSavvy Techniques

1. **Have the courage to select the best and roof the rest – eliminate unimportant tasks, reports, activities and other busy work.** You probably have the authority to "roof" some activities your team is responsible for that you determine no longer produce a valid return on investment. However, in some cases, you may have to go up the line. That will require extra courage on your part to go to *your* leader and say, "We

simply can't do it all. What do you want us to take off the table?" Remember, what your leader really wants is results. You're guaranteed better results when *your team's priorities are aligned with your leader's priorities.*

If you doubt the importance of a project or task, politely question higher-level people about the true need, value and timing of the activity. Often times, if you appropriately raise and push the issue, everyone will come to the realization that perhaps that task isn't such a priority after all.

2. Develop the habit of asking team members if their priorities are clear. After all, isn't prioritizing the team's objectives one of your key roles as a leader? Employees are often hesitant to ask leaders for help in clarifying priorities, so you must take the initiative to keep everyone focused on the essentials.

3. Make it your mission to connect individual priorities to the big picture – the organization's vision, values, history and purpose. This should be done succinctly and frequently – in meetings, memos, one-on-one sessions – and definitely anytime new work is introduced. Sharing your broader vantage point allows employees to put their work into context. If leaders will consistently connect individual priorities to organizational priorities, over time, employees will be able to more effectively prioritize on their own.

15

Set Your Beach Chair on the Sidewalk... Commit to Work-Life Balance

Picture a narrow, urban residential street at dusk. Cars line one curb. Standing on both sides are small row houses. There are no trees or flowers, only the occasional weeds growing through the cracks in the sidewalk.

Next, imagine beach chairs – lots of them, in bright colors – set in groups, here and there along the sidewalk on each side of the street. No plastic beach chairs here...only the aluminum kind with woven-fabric seats and backs. Most show the telltale signs of trips to the beach just 60 miles away on the Atlantic Ocean.

Add people to the picture: mothers, fathers, grandparents, kids, neighbors, friends. Some sit on the marble steps of the row houses; some lean against the step railings. But most sit in the beach chairs – visiting, playing Pinochle, eating roasted polly seeds (i.e., sunflower seeds)...in a word, *relaxing*.

Now listen...can you hear the children playing? The men cheering as they listen to the baseball game on the transistor radio? The women whispering about the latest neighborhood gossip? The bell ringing on the waffle man's cart as he comes down the street?

Can you smell the waffles being toasted right there on the cart... taste the cool vanilla ice cream sandwiched between two waffles sprinkled with powdered sugar?

Do you get the picture?

That is exactly how I spent many evenings of my childhood, especially during the warmer months. As soon as dinner was over, the kitchen cleaned up and the newspaper read, everyone in the neighborhood congregated outside.

To be honest, there wasn't much else to do. Kids didn't play organized sports during the week, and people didn't watch TV as much as they do today. Going out to dinner was a rare treat and attending a public sporting event or cultural affair even more special. The workday was well established – 8:00 a.m. to 5:00 p.m. – so the entire family was home in the evenings. The schedule was fairly consistent: work, housework or school in the daytime; dinner and socializing in the evening. A simple balance between "work" life and home life.

Almost half a century later, we work longer hours and take fewer vacations. Huge advances in technology have led to the practical reality that the office, the boss or clients can find us anytime, anywhere. Life itself is more complex and stressful. We've become a go-go-go society. Busy at work is followed by busy after work. Even our children are busy. All of these trends have converged to make balancing work and personal life one of the biggest challenges people face.

Let me ask you a question: Who do you think is responsible for work-life balance? Individuals? Organizations? Government? Society at large? All of the above? Ultimately, it has to come down to the individual. There's no escaping personal accountability on this issue. And yet, the organizations we work for obviously play a major role in the work-life balance challenge.

Most organizations proclaim that they value work-life balance, want their employees to experience it and want to help employees achieve it. They talk the right talk, but when it comes right down to it, their attitudes and actions send a different message. Don't believe me? If organizations and their leaders truly value work-life balance, then why do they:

- Create unrealistic deadlines that are often unnecessary?
- Demand the same (or higher!) levels of output and productivity despite reductions in staff?
- Imply through unwritten rules, snide comments, body language, voice inflection, etc., that the job ought to come first despite sick kids, weekend plans, after-work college courses and family emergencies?
- Recognize those who work harder and longer, as opposed to those who work hard and then go home and have a life?
- Expect employees to stay late or come in on weekends to finish work that genuinely can't be completed during the workday and truly isn't time critical? (Come on, unless you work at a nuclear reactor or a hospital, is the work really so vital that it can't wait?)

Why do organizations and their leaders say work-life balance is important and then behave as if it isn't?

Business.

Just as "life" often keeps us from acting on our good personal intentions such as exercising, reading, contacting an old friend or visiting Aunt Virginia in the retirement home, "business" often gets in the way of us following through on our commitment to work-life balance. There are production quotas to meet, financial statements to generate, sales to make, customers to serve. Operating the business is the top priority.

I believe the vast majority of organizations and leaders do have good intentions when it comes to work-life balance. The problem is in the follow-through, in putting those good intentions into practice. I realize leaders are under tremendous stress and pressure to produce more with less, meet deadlines, beat last year's numbers, engage employees and keep up with email, to name just a few. No one is maliciously trying to deprive employees of a personal life. You're just trying to do your job and keep your head above water. I know how you feel. I've been there too.

But we can't escape the truth: **Leaders have a major impact on the work-life balance of their employees**. You are the ones who – through your attitude and actions – create and sustain the work-life culture of your organization, whether positive or negative.

For example, do you ever discourage employees from taking off more than a few consecutive days? Is it never a "good time" to take vacation in your department? If the subtle, unspoken message of your culture is that people should not use all their personal days or vacation time, you might as well just change your policy to reflect less vacation time because that's in effect what's happening anyway.

What is your reaction when an employee takes a long lunch to go to his/her child's parent-teacher conference? How do you feel when a team member leaves at 4 p.m. once a month to play golf, even though he/she came in early to compensate? Are you supportive and encouraging? Or do you give them the "hairy eyeball" – that squinty-eyed, furrowed-brow, disapproving look?

If you are a leader of leaders, do you hold managers who report to you accountable for improving work-life balance for their teams? And do you take action with those who do the opposite? If a mid-level manager gives an employee time off to deal with a personal issue, is he/she applauded by you, HR and senior management? Or is the leader chided and criticized?

Some leaders are workaholics who expect their team members to hold the same values as they do. But I believe a lot of leaders simply aren't aware of their actions. In fact, I think a big part of the problem is that **leaders' behaviors are often unintentionally out of sync because they've never clearly defined the concept of work-life balance** within the context of their team or organization.

If work-life balance in your organization means an annual picnic and 10-minute birthday celebrations for employees, so be it. If your definition of balance is onsite childcare and four-day workweeks during the summer, fine. The act of defining work-life balance is, dare I say, almost more important than *how* you define it. Without a clear definition, the meaning of work-life balance will be left open to interpretation. And you can bet that you'll have as many different interpretations as you have employees! Ambiguous standards make for frustrated leaders and disappointed and disengaged employees when expectations aren't met. Conversely, clarity leads to improved accountability because you have benchmarks against which both employees and leaders can be held responsible.

I realize this work-life balance issue may sound like pie in the sky, but more and more organizations are waking up to the importance of balance. It wasn't too many years ago that those who went to work for management consulting firms or Wall Street investment banks could expect to work ludicrously long hours, travel extensively and spend a great deal of time away from family. But when quality candidates and existing employees began saying no to that kind of lifestyle, these organizations were forced to change their culture and their approach to work-life balance to keep from losing valuable talent.

Unfortunately, there are still too many organizations in which work-life balance is a joke…and not a funny one. It's time for organizations and their leaders to either make work-life balance a priority or stop saying it's important. Ultimately, the test of any stated policy, value or belief is in the implementation and in the behaviors and actions of those involved.

Work-life balance must become more than something that's acceptable on a temporary or short-term basis. It must become an everyday, organization-wide expectation. If that is to happen, it will require courage…courage from you and thousands of other leaders. Commit to work-life balance for yourself and for your team, whether *your* leader does or not.

Now that I've hit you between the eyes with this issue, let me tell you the good news. There are many reasons to move work-life balance closer to the top of your leadership priority list. Specifically, Your Return on Investment (YROI) is:

➢ **More productive employees.** Studies by organizations such as Gallup and Deloitte indicate that a balanced employee is a more productive employee. Furthermore, recent research confirms the connection between extended periods of stress and increases in medical claims and safety violations/accidents. Team members who are stressed, tired and overworked don't contribute to the bottom line in the medium and long term. Think about it: how much productivity do you really get from employees in their ninth or tenth hour of a shift? Are you getting their best work? Doubtful. Work-life balance is just good business sense.

➤ **Increased retention.** Work-life balance is more than just a buzzword. It's a critical factor in employee and leader retention. A-level players are leaving the corporate world in droves to start their own businesses. What's one of the most often cited reasons? Better work-life balance. Furthermore, *USA Today* reports, "Today's youngest workers are more interested in making their jobs accommodate their families and personal lives. They want jobs with flexibility, telecommuting options and the ability to go part-time or leave the workforce temporarily when children are in the picture." Leaders who are committed to work-life balance will earn the loyalty of these younger workers who don't intend to make the sacrifices their parents did for a career.

➤ **More balance for yourself and more influence in the organization.** Leaders are often hit hardest with work-life challenges. Although there certainly are hourly employees who work late or pick up extra shifts when necessary, leaders feel the squeeze the most. When you become more adept at work-life balance yourself and become an advocate for your team, your success will garner the respect of others. As productivity and retention increase, you will become the tail that wags the dog, positively influencing work-life culture throughout the organization.

The phrase "work-life balance" didn't exist back when I was a kid, but people intuitively understood its value and created it nonetheless. The streets were empty until that first person dragged out his beach chair and set it up on the pavement in front of his house. That was the signal. Soon the streets would fill with people seeking rejuvenation to face another day of challenges. We didn't know we were balancing our work and home lives. We just knew it as a way of life in which it was okay to use beach chairs where there was no beach.

How *You* Doin'?

- Do you and your organization "walk your talk" when it comes to work-life balance? Are your attitudes, actions and behaviors in sync with your stated philosophy on balancing work and personal life?

- Is putting in "face time" after hours or on weekends a requirement for promotion in your organization or on your team?

- Do your employees clearly understand what work-life balance means within the context of your team and organization? For that matter, do *you* clearly understand what it means?

- Would your team members say you are an advocate for work-life balance?

- On a scale of 1 to 10, with 10 being your ideal, how well do *you* balance work and home?

StreetSavvy Techniques

1. **Clearly define, articulate and communicate what "work-life balance" means for your team or organization.** Develop a reasonable, workable description of work-life balance for your situation and culture and then communicate, communicate, communicate. Work-life balance can be a complex, thorny issue. Regularly discuss work-life challenges at team meetings to further clarify your definition and expectations.

2. **Identify areas where your practices are out of sync with your stated intentions.** The bulleted list on page 149 is a good place to start. Go back and review it now. Are there any practices

that you or your organization may be guilty of? If so, take action to make changes within your team or department and use your influence to affect change at the organizational level.

3. **Encourage (and I don't mean *force*) employees to take all the time they've earned for vacation and personal leave.** Everyone needs time to recharge. Whether or not your company has a "use it or lose it" vacation policy, remind employees periodically throughout the year to make full use of their vacation days. Then, when they submit their requests for days off, avoid the hairy eyeball. Make every effort to accommodate their requests and do it with a positive attitude.

4. **Recognize and acknowledge those who are successful at balancing their work and personal lives.** We celebrate all kinds of things at work – getting the big deal, making quota, record profits, the launch of a new product, employment anniversaries. Why not celebrate work-life balance? Do you have employees who take care of an elderly parent, volunteer with charitable organizations, hold leadership positions in school or neighborhood associations, run in marathons? Look for team members who exemplify your organization's definition of work-life balance and make a positive example of them.

5. **Provide quality books, articles and resources about non-work-related issues.** It's common practice these days for organizations to purchase and give employees professional development books on subjects such as leadership, teamwork, communication, attitude and engagement. Why not employ the same concept to help employees improve their skills outside of the office on topics like health, stress, retirement, financial security, identity theft, etc.? You could buy copies of a particular book for each employee, start a personal

development library or bring in experts to speak during brown-bag lunches.

6. **Involve employees to find creative solutions to work-life challenges.** If you find yourself with a business challenge that is likely to affect employees' personal lives, involve your team members (and other teams/departments if necessary) in developing workable solutions that respect the work-life culture of your organization. For example, if your team is given an unexpected project with a close-in deadline, get your team together and say, "This is what needs to be done, and yet we don't want to kill ourselves in the process. What do you suggest?" One or more people on the team might volunteer to work extra shifts because they want the overtime (which improves their personal finances). Or perhaps everyone agrees to work through lunch all week long to get the project done and go home to their families on time. The result is a win/win situation in which the project is completed and work-life balance is respected.

   Many organizations are creating CARE teams that help employees in times of personal need or crisis such as serious illness/hospitalization, birth of a child, death of a family member, divorce, etc. These committees do everything from arranging for meals to assisting with finding work coverage for the employee while he/she is out.

16

Cheer for the Pomacs...
Coach Your Way to Success

Although I was fairly independent growing up, I was surrounded by mentors and advisors (in addition to my parents) who coached me. They had different titles – aunt, teacher, principal, older cousin, neighbor, store owner – but they all did the same thing, and that was to train and prepare me for life. Looking back, I realize that life never felt particularly difficult. Perhaps that was because I had the support of so many people, or maybe it was because I was receptive to their coaching. More than likely, it was a combination of both.

My dad was my earliest coach. He taught me how to swing a baseball bat (we actually started with a broom handle). He also mentored me about values and morals. Charlie, an older friend who lived across the street, helped me stay "cool." He gave me a slap on the back when I did the right thing and set me straight when I did something he thought would take me down the wrong path.

Of all the people who mentored and coached me, only one actually held the title of coach and that was Skip. (It's a wonder he survived in South Philly with a name like that. "Skip" was practically the equivalent of "a boy named Sue.") He was the coach of my baseball team, The Pomacs. In reality, he was coach, manager, trainer and equipment guy, all in one. To a bunch of teenagers, Skip seemed old, but he was probably only in his late twenties or early thirties. He was quite knowledgeable about baseball. And unlike some of the other coaches who just sat on the bench smoking cigarettes, Skip was very involved. He knew how to get the most out of us – he was quick to correct us when we made mistakes, but just as quick to recognize us when we got it right.

It's easy to see in hindsight that Skip was a great coach. At the time though, I wasn't so sure. When he first took over the team, we had a losing record. We were the ragtag team in the league. Even our name, The Pomacs, was a bit motley…most of the players lived on or near **Po**rter and Co**mac** Streets, so we just combined the names. The other teams had nicer uniforms and better equipment and were named after professional teams like the Phillies, the Yankees and the Red Sox.

After a few games, Skip decided to make some changes, including moving me to catcher. I'd always played leftfield. I was comfortable there, and I thought I was a pretty good outfielder. As you might guess, I wasn't too keen on the idea of playing catcher, and I resisted the idea. But when Skip pointed out that I could consistently catch and hold on to the ball and that the team was better off with me at catcher, I begrudgingly agreed to give it a try. As is so often the case with coaches, he was right, and we started winning more games.

Coaches are the unsung heroes of the sports world. Today, the players are the superstars, but 20 or 30 years ago, that wasn't the case. Consider the popularity back then of Vince Lombardi, Tom Landry, Lou Pinella, Lou Holtz, Joe Torre, Pat Summit, Red Auerbach, Tommy Lasorda and John Wooden.

I believe the same is true in business – coaches are the unsung heroes of the organization. Coaches bring out the best in employees and build commitment and engagement. When employees have a good coach, they deal better with priority shifts, policy adjustments, customer demands and all the other organizational changes that will inevitably occur. Coaches elevate the performance of each individual and therefore the team and ultimately the organization. There are many people in an organization who act as coaches, including trainers, facilitators, HR folks and co-workers. But without question, leaders are in the best position to coach their people, and I believe that **coaching is one of the major responsibilities of a leader.**

As a leader, you are held accountable for accomplishing a certain function – selling, producing a product, servicing clients, managing technology, tracking finances, etc. But you don't do the bulk of the work to accomplish that function – your team does. You accomplish work through other people. As a result, your performance is directly connected to their performance, and your success is tied to their success. For your employees to be successful, they must: 1) have the knowledge and skills to do their job, and 2) be aware of how well they're performing that job.

When I coach leaders to be better coaches, I distinguish between the two types of coaching:

- Coaching for problem solving;
- Coaching for performance enhancement.

Coaching for *problem solving* is the form most leaders are familiar with. An employee has a performance problem, and the leader works with him/her to resolve that problem. Coaching for *performance enhancement* – i.e., helping solid performers become even better – is far less common in business. I find that ironic because coaching for performance enhancement is the most common form of coaching in sports. Because they want to continuously improve their performance, all the top athletes have a coach (sometimes several), such as Tiger Woods and his coach, Hank Haney.

The prevailing belief in business is that coaching is only for those employees who are having trouble. The fact is that **everyone needs coaching**. Coaching is about closing performance gaps, whether you're dealing with a poor performer who has a huge gap or a star performer who needs to close the gap between 98 and 100 percent. In my 35-plus years of experience, my observation is that only about one in four leaders actively and consistently coaches employees for problem solving and performance enhancement. If coaching is one of a leader's top priorities, I'd say we have a significant performance gap! We'd better get some coaching!

Why don't more leaders coach their employees? I believe there are several reasons:

> ➢ **Coaching is contradictory to what leaders do best**. By definition, leaders are rewarded for taking charge, solving problems, acting quickly and analyzing situations with minimal information. Coaching involves two-way communication, lots of patience, letting the individual take responsibility for solving the problem and getting all the facts before moving forward.

> ➢ **Coaching isn't easy**. Many people simply don't like to confront or criticize other people, and they certainly don't want to discipline them (the most serious kind of coaching). In *The Manager's Coaching Handbook*, author David Cottrell says, "Coaching is not a popularity contest. Coaching is about enhancing your team's performance. Everyone likes to be liked, but that shouldn't be your

first priority. As a leader, one of your most important responsibilities is to effect change. And people typically resist change. Be ready to acquire more than a few critics and detractors as you coach your team to success. But you'll soon discover, if you haven't already, that the best way to earn respect is to help others succeed." Sure, coaching can involve some uncomfortable moments, but *if it's done timely and correctly,* coaching becomes more about building relationships than dealing with performance problems.

➢ **Leaders think coaching doesn't work**. I've had countless leaders tell me that they coached their people, but their performance didn't improve. When we get down to the nitty-gritty, I almost always discover that these leaders *told* the individuals what to do to solve the problem. These leaders followed the athletic-coaching model, which is primarily one-way coaching – the coach tells the athlete exactly what to do to improve and doesn't ask for the athlete's opinion or input. This approach doesn't work in the business world because it leaves "ownership" of the problem with the leader instead of with the employee where it belongs. If done correctly, coaching produces dramatic results. **Effective coaching is a two-way, participatory process which results in the individual understanding the issue and its impact, accepting ownership of the problem and making a commitment to change.**

➢ **Too often, leaders aren't held accountable for coaching employees**. I know I sound like a broken record (the grandfather of the CD) when it comes to accountability. But if you look at a typical performance appraisal form for a leader, you'll find nothing about coaching employees. And if it's not on the performance appraisal form, I guarantee there's no accountability for it. The irony is that it does appear on most 360° assessments. Sure, it may be more difficult for the boss to evaluate coaching skills than the leader's direct reports, but it can be done by looking at outcomes and results.

➢ **Leaders are busy.** This is what I hear from leaders in the trenches – that they're just too busy and too overwhelmed to coach their people. But coaching is a prime example of short-term investment for long-term gain. So much of leadership success is simply about being focused on the long term. Leadership expert and author Lee Colan says, "Coaching is a pay-me-now or pay-me-later leadership proposition. Take a shortcut, and you'll be saying the same thing to the same employee next week. Excellent leaders invest their time on coaching right the first time, and as a result, prevent re-coaching. Coach them now or coach them later…the choice is yours."

➢ **Leaders don't have adequate coaching skills.** Notice I said *skills*, not *ability*. There's a big difference. Very few people are naturally good coaches, so most of us need training. Your employees truly want to know how they are performing, but they don't want to be brutalized in the process. Using good coaching technique is crucial. It can mean the difference between solving a problem and further entrenching a problem; between committed, engaged employees and distrustful, disengaged employees.

So let's get real…with all these obstacles and challenges, why should you bother to coach your people?

Because *your* success depends on it. It's that simple.

When you consistently coach employees for both problem solving *and* performance enhancement, you will quickly develop a reputation as a leader who gets exceptional results and who employees want to work for. And that means more accolades, recognition and success for you.

How *You* Doin'?

- Do you coach the people on your team? If so, do you coach them in the often-forgotten area of performance enhancement, or do you coach them only when there are problems?

- When you coach, do you tell the employee what to do to improve and therefore end up "owning" the problem?

- Are you coached by *your* leader for both problem solving and performance enhancement? If not, what can you do to change that situation?

StreetSavvy Techniques

1. **Address performance gaps early**. I can't stress this enough. As Nike says, "Just do it!" When you address problems early – as soon as you become aware of them – coaching is easier on everyone. First, problems are just plain easier to solve when they're caught early before they become serious. The longer a behavior continues, the more likely it will become a habit that is harder to change. Second, when you address a problem early, the coaching session itself is much more pleasant for both you and the employee. You have the opportunity to support the employee and say, "Let's discuss this issue so you can address it before it becomes a more serious problem."

And finally, I'll go so far as to say that withholding information about an employee's performance is unethical. It's simply not fair or acceptable to tell an employee he or she has had a performance gap for weeks or months, especially one that could affect his or her compensation, promotion potential or employment status. Don't put yourself in the extremely uncomfortable position of having to explain to the employee and to your boss why you waited six months to bring a performance problem to the employee's attention.

2. **Invest the time to effectively coach team members.** Yes, I know you're busy. And again, not only is coaching one of your top priorities as a leader, but it is also the best way to ensure your own success. A small investment of time now will pay big dividends in the future.

3. **Always remember that coaching is a participatory, two-way street**. That means, first and foremost, that a good coach listens more than he/she talks. A good target to shoot for is 40/60 – you talk 40 percent, the employee talks 60 percent. (By the way, world-class coaches adhere to a 20/80 ratio.) If you're doing all the talking, there's no chance for the employee to explain, which often means you may not be discussing the true cause of the issue.

4. **Get some training.** Most people are not naturally good coaches, so most of us need training. Unfortunately, too few organizations offer their leaders effective coaching-skills training. The best coaching training is hands-on, role-play training, rather than note-taking lectures. If your organization doesn't provide coaching-skills training, look for outside programs or visit www.ADLAssociates.com for coaching resources.

5. **Follow this proven coaching model.** Follow these proven, time-tested techniques for both types of coaching every time you have a coaching session with an employee:

   Step 1: Gap. Identify the problem (coaching for problem solving) or the gap in performance (coaching for performance enhancement) clearly and very specifically. Talk only about specific, observable behaviors and facts, and stay away from generalities, opinions, judgments and labels. Establish and define the true issue – what the employee *is* doing versus what the employee *needs to be* doing.

   For example, assume you are a cashier supervisor at a retail store, and one of your cashiers is not exhibiting the level of customer service you expect. Your coaching session with that employee would start like this: "Chris, this is what I've observed. You are, in fact, scanning items and checking people out. However, you are not providing the level of service we strive to give our customers because you are not smiling, saying hello, speaking courteously to or interacting with the customers."

   Step 2: Explanation. Next, ask an open-ended question that will get the employee talking about why he/she thinks the problem or gap is occurring. For example, "Chris, I'd like to hear your thoughts on this issue." Your tone of voice and word choice are incredibly important in coaching. Saying something like, "What do you have to say about this?" isn't conducive to getting the employee to open up to you.

Now...shut up! Practice the 40/60 talking/listening rule. You absolutely *must* find out what the employee perceives is the cause of the problem. In our example, there could be many possible causes for the performance gap. One might be that the cashier is experiencing personal problems that are impacting her work, and she was simply unaware of her demeanor. Or perhaps the store manager mentioned in a meeting that customer wait-times have been too long and cashiers need to move people through the line more quickly. Maybe the store is understaffed, and she's working double shifts to cover for other employees. Or perhaps she simply doesn't have the necessary customer service skills.

As a leader, you may think you know what's going on, but you can't know for sure unless you listen to the individual. If you guess the cause of the problem and you're wrong, the problem will continue. Likewise, if you tell the employee why he/she has the problem (e.g., "You're not friendly with the customers because you have a bad attitude"), I can virtually guarantee failure.

These first two coaching steps are critical. If you do these well, often times the rest almost falls into place. If you don't do these steps well, you may alienate the individual or focus on the wrong problem.

Step 3: **Impact.** This is the statement that tells the employee why his/her behavior matters. When coaching for performance enhancement, outline the positive impact of improving performance. For problem solving, clearly identify the negative effects and the magnitude of the behavior. In other words, explain the impact of the behavior on customers, safety, quality, production, etc. *Don't* discuss the impact on the employee, such as, "If this behavior continues, you will face formal discipline." If the situation is affecting other employees, be sure to address it. People often can't emotionally connect with the idea that their actions affect profit. But when they discover their behaviors are causing their co-workers difficulty or hardship, it can be a powerful motivator to change.

To the cashier, your impact statement might be something like, "Chris, often times you are the only person our customers come in contact with. Therefore, the feelings they have about our entire establishment and their desire to come back will be based solely on their interaction with you."

Let impact be your guide to the seriousness of the problem. Is chewing gum a problem? It depends. If an employee does data entry at a computer all day long, it's not really an issue. If the employee is a receptionist and customers can't understand her, it's clearly a problem. Sometimes discussing impact won't be necessary, as when the employee tells you information that requires more investigation (such as discussing with the store manager how to balance wait-times with exceptional service) or the employee quickly states that he/she didn't realize the behavior was a problem and immediately commits to changing. In these cases, there's no point to beating the employee down by discussing impact.

Step 4: **Solution.** Ask the employee for his/her solution to the issue. One of the biggest mistakes leaders make in coaching is giving the employee the solution. That puts ownership of the problem and the solution squarely on the leader's shoulders – exactly where it *doesn't* belong. To ensure employee ownership of the solution – and therefore commitment to implement that solution – the employee must develop the action that will work for him/her. If you dictate the solution, it's too easy for the employee to say it didn't work.

Ask an open-ended question such as, "What do you believe you can do to close the gap or resolve the issue?" and then *listen*! If the employee can't come up with a potential solution, resist the urge to supply one! Instead say, "I realize you may need some time to develop a solution. Think about it overnight and let's talk again tomorrow."

Step 5: **Commitments.** Note the "s" on the end of the word. Coaching involves a commitment from the employee and also a commitment from you. Although it may seem obvious that the employee will implement the solution, I believe it's essential to gain the individual's specific commitment to enhance his/her performance or resolve the issue: "Chris, you've told me your proposed solution. Will you do this, and are there any obstacles that would prevent you from doing it?"

Your clerk might answer with, "Yes, I will go back and review my training manual and focus on interacting more with the customers. And yet, if I get pressured to get the line moving fast, this may happen again."

As the coach, your commitment is two-fold. First, you should commit to remove any obstacles or barriers to the employee's success: "I will do the best I can to minimize that pressure. If it does happen, please let me know immediately." Second, you must commit to follow up with the employee and give him/her feedback: "Chris, I'll follow up with you on this in one week to give you some feedback about your progress."

Step 6: **Feedback and recognition**. Follow up regularly and consistently to provide the employee with feedback on progress. Recognize positive changes that indicate the employee is moving in the right direction, even if he/she hasn't yet achieved your expected level of performance. A key element of coaching is acknowledging and reinforcing *incremental* improvement.

Some leaders mistakenly think they should *only* acknowledge the complete elimination of the performance gap or results that are 100 percent in alignment with expectations. That would be like not recognizing a baby who is learning to walk until he/she is able to run. Just as a young child needs encouragement throughout the process of crawling, pulling up, standing, taking tentative steps and finally walking on her own, employees need feedback and recognition that they are on the right path to performance improvement. Acknowledge positive incremental effort, attitude and action, and you'll see permanent change much more quickly.

If after several *quality* coaching sessions, an employee refuses to accept ownership of the problem or fails to adequately close the performance gap, it's time to consider formal discipline or possibly termination.

Remember: Being a good coach takes practice. It's a lot like golf – you don't become great with just one lesson or one day on the course.

17

Check Out the New Kid on the Block...
Address Cultural Fit Problems Early

When I think back on my days growing up in South Philly, one of my clearest memories is how tight-knit the people in our neighborhood were. As an adult, I feel sorry for the new kids that had to move into our neighborhood. It wasn't easy being the new kid on the block, and there was no way you'd be accepted if you didn't fit in with the crowd. We didn't harass kids if they didn't fit it in; we simply didn't include them in our conversations or invite them to play Halfball or Dead Box. What can I say? Kids aren't always the nicest people.

The idea of not accepting people into a group has a lot of negative implications, and it's certainly not one I agree with. And yet, if one looks at it objectively, it did serve a purpose – it maintained the culture of our neighborhood. And if we consciously choose to find the positive in every situation, we will discover there is indeed a StreetSavvy Lesson here for organizations that want to maintain a strong, solid culture and employer brand.

What do you do when someone new "moves in" to your organization?

Years ago, many organizations had probationary periods during which new employees had to "prove" themselves. At the end of the probationary period, the new employee's performance was evaluated, and he or she was invited to stay or invited to leave. Today, some companies have introductory periods that are informal, watered-down versions of probationary periods. But for the most part, organizations have gotten away from this whole notion of a "test period" for new employees.

What a huge mistake!

Am I old fashioned? No. I'm realistic…and honest!

All too often, we find ourselves with new employees who possess the technical skills to get the job done, but something about them doesn't fit with our culture. So what do we do? Nine times out of ten, we keep them! We ignore the cultural mismatch and go on as if it has no bearing on the team or on results.

The most important factor in a new employee's success in your organization is something you cannot discover through interview questions, uncover with references, identify in personality tests or observe in a group interview. What is this essential factor? *How that individual will actually function in your unique environment* – on your team, subject to your policies, within your processes, under your pressures, in your culture. It's something you can never know with certainty until that person joins and works within your organization.

Many companies aren't as StreetSavvy as they could be when it comes to this issue of cultural mismatch. On the streets of South Philly, if you weren't loyal or you didn't have the right attitude or you couldn't get along with others, you were excluded from the crowd. If you thought Halfball was stupid, you were outta' there. You just didn't fit with our group. If we could see the downsides of a cultural mismatch, why don't organizations and their leaders understand them?

> **They rationalize that the most essential part of the job is getting done.** Because the technical part of the job is, after all, the most important thing, right? Not! Here's the truth: **Employees who negatively affect the culture of the organization have a negative impact on the bottom line.** Can you remember co-workers who you really didn't enjoy working with? More than likely, it was their personal qualities and characteristics that made them difficult to work with. Perhaps they were unpleasant with customers, had a bad attitude or refused to cooperate with or help fellow teammates. Whatever the behavior, I'd bet it had a negative effect on the team's morale and productivity. Great technical skills plus poor cultural fit equals a net loss.

> **We don't want to admit that we made a hiring mistake.** Sometimes we miss the warning signs during the selection process. Other times, one person shows up for the interview, but someone completely different shows up the first day on the job. Acknowledging that a new employee isn't working out means we have to go through the time, trouble and expense to interview, hire and train someone else. So we tend to ignore the signs of trouble and hope the situation will somehow get better. Job skills can be improved over time with training. But attitude, enthusiasm and cooperation rarely improve with training. In fact, these qualities typically only get worse as time goes on.

Let me ask you this: Do you have any employees on your team who adequately perform the operational aspects of the job, but lack the qualities essential to your corporate culture – characteristics like cooperation, effective communication, teamwork or a good work ethic? Does the fact that they're not a cultural fit impact your team's attitude, productivity or results?

I'll answer that for you with one word that Rocky Balboa used a lot…"Abso*lu*tely!"

Do you ever secretly wish that you hadn't hired them in the first place? (Be totally honest.)

That's what I thought.

And that's precisely why you should have some time period in which you evaluate new employees' overall fit with the company. It doesn't matter what you call it – a probationary period, an introductory period or even a trial period. Just do it!

New employees put their best foot forward during an introductory period. If that isn't good enough, what do you think is coming next? At the end of the introductory period, if a new employee does not *enhance* your culture and add value to your team in every way, you must have the foresight and the courage to let him or her go. Cut your losses quickly and find another employee who will fit – in all respects – with your organization. When in doubt, you must show them out.

Too harsh for you? Consider the people who have to put up with this new ineffective, uncooperative, uncommunicative employee. Your existing employees who contribute positively to your culture are the first ones to identify a cultural mismatch, and they want you to do something about it. What kind of message does it send to them if you allow a new employee to get by with "cultural violations" from the get-go?

And trust me, terminating new employees who are cultural mismatches is good for *you*, the leader. It saves you a tremendous amount of time, energy and aggravation in the long run. That's the YROI, the big payoff. You'll spend far more time dealing with and coaching these employees' negative attitudes and cultural violations than starting the selection process all over again to find someone who fits.

Rita Bailey spent more than 25 years with Southwest Airlines, most recently as Director of the University for People, before leaving to start her own company. She once told me, "At Southwest, we hired for attitude, and we fired for attitude."

She went on to explain, "People often asked me how a company can fire for attitude. If a cultural standard is critical to your organization's success, you have to attach specific, identifiable behaviors to that standard. When you do that, you can hold people accountable for the behavior. For example, it's not enough to have an expectation of a 'positive attitude.' You must define what that means with unambiguous behaviors." Rita also pointed out that many organizations on *Fortune Magazine*'s list of "100 Best Companies to Work For" share a common characteristic: they attach specific behaviors to cultural standards, thereby creating accountability for those standards.

You know, I remember this kid who moved into our neighborhood in Philly. Nice enough guy and a good ballplayer, too. He added depth and skill to our street team. But for some reason, he never completely meshed with the rest of us. It wasn't that we didn't like him or he us. We just didn't click. After awhile, he came around less and less, until finally he stopped hanging out with us altogether. Then one day, I saw him playing ball with another group of kids a few blocks away. I could see that he was more comfortable with them, and together, they made a great team. He was happier with those other kids, and our group was happier and better without him.

Everyone has a "home" – a neighborhood, organization or team – where they fit in, where they belong, and where they can make a positive contribution. I believe that one of the more rewarding roles of a leader is helping people find the place where they fit. Occasionally, you'll discover that new employees aren't in sync with your team or organization. When that happens, the most respectful and caring thing you can do is to help them find a new home.

How *You* Doin'?

- Do you have employees who you knew in their first few months were not a good fit with your culture?

- Are you still paying the price for not helping them find another home early on?

- How much time do you spend coaching employees on the cultural aspects versus the technical aspects of their jobs?

StreetSavvy Techniques

1. Realistically expand your written job descriptions to include the personal qualities and characteristics that are essential to adequate performance on the job and to maintaining your culture. Go beyond the basic job skills (e.g., widget production) and get to the intangibles that have a direct effect on the job and other people on the team. Good interpersonal skills, respect for others, effective communication and teamwork might be a good start.

Then, as Rita Bailey suggests, define those qualities and attach specific, identifiable behaviors to them. Make sure these cultural job requirements are explained to new employees just as clearly as the technical requirements. And finally, don't forget to hold employees accountable to the specific behaviors.

2. Ask for input and feedback from those who work with new hires. Conduct an informal mini-360° evaluation at the end of the initial period. Who better to gauge new employees' fit with the team and the organization than their teammates? Premium grocer Whole Foods offers a great example of this approach. According to an article entitled "Worker Loyalty Takes More Than Money" that appeared in *The Dallas Morning News,* "At Whole Foods, team members vote on whether a new hire stays or goes after a four-week trial; the trainee needs two-thirds support to join the staff permanently."

3. Be prudent. Follow your attorney's advice about documentation and take the precautions you feel are necessary. But...don't allow a new employee who isn't the right fit to contaminate your positive culture. Think of it this way: You are giving this person an opportunity to find a position in another organization that better suits his/her personality, needs and career aspirations at this point in time.

18

Trade Your Rags for Pots and Pans... Swap Your Old "Stuff" for Something Better

The streets of South Philadelphia bustled with activity during the spring, summer and fall months of my childhood. It seemed like every day held a new parade of vendors plying their wares from pushcarts or small trucks up and down the narrow streets.

Some vendors we knew by name. Ernie the Insurance Man, dressed in a suit, came around once a week to collect the ten-cent life insurance premium. There were the regulars, like John the Milkman and Frank the Fruit Vendor. Other vendors we knew by sound or smell. The singing egg man announced his arrival with a different song every day, and no one could ignore the noise of the knife sharpener (who also doubled as the umbrella repair man) as he did his work on a machine right there on his cart. Our favorite, of course, was the waffle man in his big white chef's hat. We could hear his bell and smell the freshly toasted waffles at least a block away. By the time his cart rolled down our block, there'd be a group of kids eagerly waiting to buy a waffle and ice cream sandwich.

Depending on how many vendors were on the street at any given time, the air would be filled with a chorus of chants. "Javela

Water! Get your Javela Water!" in an Italian accent mixed with, "Clothes props! Clothes props!" in a young man's baritone voice. Javela Water was liquid laundry detergent sold by the gallon (although to me, it looked like plain soapy water), and a clothes prop was a seven-foot wooden pole with a "V" at the top designed to support a clothesline so the clothes wouldn't drag on the ground.

But the call that always stood out in my mind was, "Rags for pots or pans! Rags for pots or pans!" from the vendor who came down our street every few weeks. As a small child, I had no idea what he was saying, and even after I figured it out years later, I still had no idea what he was offering. It turned out to be fairly simple: he exchanged new items for old items, mostly new pots and pans for old clothes. (And to this day, I have no idea what he did with all those old clothes.) The Rag Man, as we called him, was a one-man rolling flea market.

As long as I live, I will never forget the day I was playing in front of our house, and he came ambling down the street. My mother was out front too, scrubbing the marble steps. When he got close, he called out, "Rags for pots or pans, Mrs. Lucia?" Without missing a beat, my mother fired back, "Not today…I'm wearing them!"

The Rag Man provided a tremendous service: the opportunity to swap your old, worn-out stuff for new stuff that would likely serve you better. As I think about it now, the fact that he came around fairly frequently and that people swapped a lot with him seems odd to me, because in South Philly, we weren't keen on trading in the old for the new. In fact, we were downright provincial! We were willing to exchange our old clothes for something new, better and more valuable, and yet we weren't willing to do the same with our habits, attitudes and beliefs. We were, quite frankly, narrow-minded.

For example, we summarily rejected, and perhaps even feared, anything that was new or "outside" our culture. Ideas, languages, lifestyles, food, clothing, celebrations...all cultural choices had to be "Philly." If it wasn't from South Philly or Philly proper, we viewed it with total skepticism. If it wasn't familiar, as we used to say, "Fugettaboutit!" After all, how could anything that came from someone who didn't eat cheesesteaks or root for the Phillies or the Eagles have any merit whatsoever?

We even considered the people who lived in the suburbs to be outsiders. I had an aunt and uncle and several cousins who lived in the suburbs. They had more money and took nicer vacations than we did, but we rationalized that we were somehow better than they were...they probably didn't help one another like we did or have nearly as much fun. Unbelievably, they bought their milk, eggs and fruit from a grocery store instead of from street vendors. And clearly they weren't as friendly as we were because you never saw beach chairs on their sidewalks in the evenings!

Maybe a psychologist could better explain this extremely provincial attitude, but my guess is that we simply loved our way of life and were comfortable with it. We didn't want new and different ideas to disturb what we had worked so hard to create.

Interestingly, there is often a similar provincialism in organizations - provincialism in the sense that some organizations can be narrow-minded when it comes to new ideas and ways of doing things. Many companies cling to the familiar and resist innovations that could lead to improvements in critical areas. They discount the need for new approaches, processes and methods and reject outside ideas, concepts and strategies simply because they are different and unfamiliar.

Let me guess what you're thinking right now: "No way, Al. This is the 21st century. We operate in a technology-driven, global economy that's all about change, change, change. There's no way organizations could be provincial and survive in today's marketplace."

You can believe that if you want to, but I'm going to give you the straight skinny. Organizations – and people too, for that matter – can be simultaneously forward thinking in one respect and stodgily outdated in another. An organization might reach out for the latest technology in some areas (usually those *not* as critical to core operations), while being very conservative in others (often the areas perceived to be critical to success).

I don't know of a single organization (and I've worked with quite a few and studied a whole lot more) that doesn't have what my colleague Brian Gareau calls a scotoma, more commonly known as a blind spot. Today's organizations are indeed progressive in many ways. But invariably, they also have blind spots – areas of their business where they are stuck in the old, "tried and true" methods of operating. They use processes that have remained unchanged for years because of a "that's the way we've always done it…and it's worked" mentality. And really, who can blame them? After all, they've had some measure of success doing "what they've always done" or they wouldn't still be in business.

I have a client that has been in business, quite successfully, for more than 50 years. They are a leader in their market niche and have progressive marketing and customer service strategies. Although they have a quality product, they've just recently begun to consider a formal quality process for the first time in their history. When they brought me in to assist them, their senior leadership in effect asked, "Why should we change? Why get bogged down in this quality stuff?" And even once we got past that hurdle, they were still hesitant to adopt Six Sigma or any of its permutations because they perceived those are initiatives undertaken by organizations in "other" industries. This company, forward thinking in so many ways, was limited because of its blind spot.

Through the years, I've observed that some organizations are overtly provincial, while others are unconsciously narrow-minded. There are also companies that are initially progressive, but then slip backward. They may upgrade to the newest technology or implement the hottest management craze, but sooner or later, they slowly gravitate back to their comfort zones. Even organizations that utilize outside experts can be insular. Many either flat-out ignore consultants' recommendations or adopt them for a short time and then revert to their old ways.

Provincialism isn't unique to organizations. In fact, I've found that industry provincialism is often even stronger. I've lost track of how many times I've shared best practices with a client, only to have the ideas rejected because they didn't come from the client's industry. (Actually, when it comes to the people side of business, there are actually far more similarities than differences between industries. People are people and tend to have the same issues and challenges no matter where they work or what they do.)

Teams and departments can also display "silo mentality," refusing to benchmark other successful groups within the organization due to what I call "disciplinary snobbery" – when pride in one's discipline or functional area keeps you from learning across departmental lines. What could the IT department possibly learn from marketing and sales?

Generational differences are yet another example of narrow-mindedness. Employees in different generations tend to have a limited outlook, appreciating their own generational "culture" while rejecting the ideas, values, work styles and methods of employees from other generations. (For more about generational differences, see Chapter 6.)

And now it comes down to you, the leaders. You may not want to admit it, but you can be provincial too. Yes, it's true – there are thousands of leaders in Corporate America today who refuse to recognize the value of diversity and inclusion or who stubbornly believe that employee turnover has no effect on the bottom line. Many leaders won't get onboard with coaching and instead continue to tell their employees exactly what to do and when to do it in no uncertain terms. There are leaders who still hold firm to the belief that recognition is for "softies." They don't believe in recognition, they don't think they need it, and they certainly aren't going to give it.

So what would organizational behavioralists say are the reasons behind corporate provincialism? Who knows? But I'll certainly give you my perspective. First, it's simply human nature to want to stay in our comfort zone, to stick with that which is known and familiar. We tend to fear being different or being "the first." Companies often talk about being leaders in their industry, but most aren't willing to actually step out and do it, choosing instead to follow common industry practices.

A number of years ago, I worked with a company in the steel industry. One might think that a dirty-fingernail kind of company whose products date back to the industrial revolution might be somewhat unsophisticated. But this organization was quite the opposite. It chose to embrace progressive ideas from outside its industry. While virtually all of the other companies in the industry were unionized, it was non-union and wanted to keep it that way.

Senior leadership could have stuck their heads in the sand and hoped that the things they'd done in the past to keep them union-free would continue to work. Instead, they brought in my organization to help them implement what was back then a revolutionary approach to labor relations – a peer-based dispute resolution process (still considered progressive by many today). The payoff for their forward thinking included fewer grievances, lower turnover, a less hostile work environment and a continued union-free workplace.

The leaders in this particular organization had courage. And to be totally honest, courageous leadership is lacking in many organizations. Leaders are inclined to follow their organization's accepted practices because it's safer and easier on their careers. They often earn their title by being the best in their area of expertise, so they tend to stick with what got them promoted in the first place.

Furthermore, in some organizations, leaders have learned the hard way that they'll get kicked in the pants if they try something different and it fails. In fact, there's often little reward for trying new ideas unless the results are phenomenally successful. Sure, organizations often talk about valuing creativity and innovation. But what they really mean is, "Give us only those ideas that you've researched and documented the possible outcomes and that will generate a ten percent return on investment in the first two years." It's not that they are disingenuous; it's that the marketplace is cutthroat. If a new idea or concept isn't guaranteed to be bankable, it's safer to stick with the status quo.

The level of provincialism varies dramatically from company to company and from leader to leader. Adopting a new process, changing a long-standing business practice or upgrading to a new technology can be risky. But in today's business climate, it's even riskier to ignore outside ideas and processes that could significantly benefit you and your organization.

To be clear, I'm not advocating that you manage by best seller or jump on the latest business fad. Being open to thought-provoking concepts and strategies is a far cry from implementing every new idea that comes along. We may never again hear a street vendor calling, "Rags for pots or pans," but we ought to be StreetSavvy enough to swap our "old stuff' for something better. It's time to get rid of old attitudes, thoughts and processes, and trade them in for new ones that will likely be far more valuable.

There are very few things I'd change about the way I grew up. But one thing I'd definitely change would be our rejection of outside ideas in the name of Philly loyalty. It wasn't loyalty! It was small mindedness and it was limiting. I don't miss it. I realize now that adhering to a strict, limited view can actually destroy something we love by choking out new ideas.

If you love your organization "just the way it is," be careful...you might just love it to death!

How *You* Doin'?

- Do you reject different ideas, concepts or processes merely because they are just that...*different?*

- Do you keep up with best practices from other departments, competitor organizations and other industries, and keep an open mind about implementing them?

- Do you encourage or discourage your team to consider fresh approaches to continuous improvement? For that matter, do you believe in continuous improvement?

StreetSavvy Techniques

1. **Identify your blind spots.** One of the most important things you can do is develop awareness about your organizational and leadership blind spots. Everyone has them…it's part of being human. Your blind spots are likely the areas where you tend to be provincial. These are the same areas that could benefit the most from some updated thinking.

2. **Evaluate your "slippage."** Make a list of new concepts, initiatives or processes that your team or department has implemented over the last few years. Then identify those instances where you've slipped back to the old way of doing things and determine why it happened. Was it because the old way truly is better or because the old way is easier and more comfortable? Think about this: obviously the new idea was deemed good enough for you to invest the time, money and resources to make a switch in the first place. What's changed?

3. **Adopt a "we'll try just about anything once" mentality.** Force yourself not to immediately discount or judge ideas from your team members. Recognize employees for their creativity and innovation, and ask them to put together a *basic* analysis or report that describes how this idea represents an improvement over your current process. Then ask the rest of the team for their inputs and upgrades.

   If it seems feasible and wouldn't create any significant, long-term problems if it were to fail, give it a try. This is especially practical when you're not facing a deadline or there won't be major consequences for a less-than-perfect outcome. Chances are, you'll discover more things that don't work than do, but I guarantee you'll learn something beneficial from every single experience that can be applied to your business.

If this idea of "try anything once" seems way out there to you, think about times in your life when you took some "outside" advice – professionally or personally – and it worked out well for you. Why not try it again? The way you've always done it may be comfortable, but it also may be limiting your success.

4. Combat provincialism one step at a time. Be progressive in a non-revolutionary way. In other words, ease in to big new changes. Charging forward to quickly implement sweeping changes can create strong resistance and entrench provincialism even more. Don't bite off more than you can chew. Sometimes, *slow is fast*. (Think about that one for a minute or two!) Make changes in a planned, purposeful manner with a high degree of honesty and respect for employees.

5. "Get outta' Philly!" That's my way of saying, "Look outward for valuable new ideas." Ask your team members to identify a challenge your team is facing. Then have everyone on the team do some research and networking to find potential solutions that your team has never tried before. Professional associations are a great place to go for benchmarking opportunities. Another option is to solicit proposals from outside experts. You'll be amazed at the possibilities that exist "out there."

19

Change "The Way You Do the Things You Do"... Get Bigger Returns for the Same Investment of Time

Everywhere you went in Philadelphia in the 1950s and 60s you heard great music…emanating from bars and restaurants, playing on every phonograph while parents were out and blasting from transistor radios (the diminutive parents of boom boxes and the clunky grandparents of MP3 players).

Music played a big part in our lives. It was a source of entertainment, a means of expression, and it made for an upbeat (pun intended) atmosphere. My most vivid memories of music came from the streets. That's right, the streets! It seemed like every street corner was home to an a cappella (without instruments) group. In fact, Frankie Avalon and Fabian are both from South Philly and were "discovered" singing on street corners.

Three of my buddies (Frank Fienberg, Joel Leson and Danny Salvano) and I had our own little doo-wop group. Although none of us were a Frankie or Fabian, we sounded pretty good. We used to make up our own songs, usually about unrequited teenage love. I can still remember the lyrics and tune of one song to this very day:

Why Didn't You Tell Me?

Bum Ba Diddily
Bum Ba Diddily
Bum Ba Diddily
Yip, Yip

Bum Ba Diddily
Bum Ba Diddily
Bum Ba Diddily
Yip, Yip

Why didn't you tell me?
Why didn't you say?
Why didn't you answer?
When I asked about yesterday?

I thought you loved me
But I guess it's not that way…ay

Repeat Bum Ba Diddilies and Yip Yips

Other than our original works, my favorite songs were "Come Go With Me" by the Del Vikings and "Chances Are" by Johnny Mathis. Some years later, I enjoyed singing "The Way You Do the Things You Do" by the Temptations. It was a fun song that over the years developed a deeper meaning. The lyrics are all about wooing a female. But if you just think about the phrase *the way you do the things you do*, this song can represent an important lesson for today's busy leaders.

One of the major complaints I hear from leaders is that they just don't have time in their already maxed-out schedules to focus on the "people" aspects of their job – building trust, developing relationships, coaching, giving recognition, communicating, listening, showing concern, etc. I concur. I see too many leaders who are indifferent, sarcastic, even rude, because they are so stressed out, focused on the bottom line or caught in a deadline crunch. I guess "the way they do the things they do" is to meet the operational objectives and let the people objectives be damned.

There are a few leaders who are just ogres…and proud of it! And certainly many managers simply aren't aware of how they come across to employees (just another reason why 360-degree feedback, formal or informal, is so critical). But many leaders feel justified in skipping the niceties of basic human kindness and respect with their employees because of pressures and time constraints. I believe these leaders view time somewhat simplistically and tend to think only about the short-term perspective. As a result, they won't invest time in something they perceive may not have an immediate payoff. What they fail to consider, however, are the medium- and long-term effects of *not* making that investment of time in people issues.

For example, I'm amazed when leaders tell me they don't have time to coach or mentor team members. Apparently they haven't thought about the truly tremendous amount of time required to continuously deal with those employees and their problems over and over and over again…issues that likely could be resolved with a few 30-minute coaching sessions.

Then there are managers who can't find the time to adequately build a relationship with a new employee. But what happens when that employee quits within the first year because he/she doesn't feel valued? That same leader who couldn't spare a few hours now has to spend perhaps 40 or 50 hours to recruit, hire and train a replacement. And that doesn't take into account the time involved with losing an employee, such as reassigning responsibilities or covering shifts.

There's no doubt leaders are busy. I don't question that. I do, however, question the logic behind de-valuing, de-emphasizing or flat-out ignoring interpersonal connections between leaders and employees. It seems that many leaders either don't know or have forgotten that how they treat employees affects performance and therefore the very results they want. A study by The Saratoga Institute – the premier organization for measuring the ROI of human capital – indicates that people who feel respected and fulfilled at work are not only more productive, but also provide better customer service.

Furthermore, according to Metrus Group, an industry leader in strategic performance measurement and organizational assessment, "The evidence that people issues influence profit is hard to refute. Just about every piece of research conducted over the last ten years has come to this conclusion: Organizations with leaders who treat people with respect and use their people skills wisely are likely to retain committed employees who are willing to go the extra mile. Employee retention and commitment lead to higher customer retention, higher productivity, increased quality, and continuous improvement. Companies whose leaders do not do well on people issues experience high employee turnover, psychological withdrawal, lack of customer focus, and poorly motivated employees. These are customer service and high-performance killers."

So what is a busy leader to do? How are you supposed to meet operational goals and add people goals as well? How can you juggle even more balls or spin even more plates than you already are?

Rather than seeing the people side of business as an add-on to the things you already do, I suggest you reframe it and view it as the *way* you do the things you do. In other words, focus on people while you do the things you're already doing. The truth is, the vast majority of people-oriented activities can be piggybacked onto or combined with your existing tasks, projects, meetings, assignments, one-on-ones, etc. Instead of spending more *time* on people-focused activities, I'm suggesting more *intent*. This is one of those rare situations when multitasking actually works.

There are plenty of organizations that pay careful attention to the way they do the things they do. Each year, my organization, ADL Associates, hosts and sponsors an HR Executive Forum. At one recent Forum, held at a well-known hotel, a human resource executive from the same hotel chain was a Forum participant. During one of the sessions, she described her organization's high level of employee engagement. I decided to see for myself if what she was saying was true. So I asked an employee who was refilling the coffee urns how he felt about his company. Without hesitation and with a genuine smile on his face, he told me that he'd been with the company eight years and that he'd recommended the organization to others because he was treated with respect and was encouraged to enjoy his work. This organization prides itself on the way it treats its employees. It's no surprise to me that they regularly appear on *Fortune* magazine's list of Best Companies in America to Work For.

What about you…do you think front-line service employees who stay with an organization for eight years and genuinely enjoy their job are beneficial? Do you think this organization's focus on the people side of business positively affects its bottom line?

The benefit of dovetailing people-focused activities with operational activities is clear: **higher returns for the *same* amount of time invested.** Higher productivity, better results, increased profit – all with no additional time on your part. That's a no-brainer and a great YROI!

The Singing Egg Man is a great example of this ROI. When I was a kid back in Philly, many staples, including eggs, were delivered to our door rather than purchased at the market. The egg delivery man provided good service to begin with. He knew every customer by name – and often the names of their husbands and children too – and he rarely fouled up an order. But that wasn't what made him exceptional. He was unique because he sang *while* he went about his deliveries. And I don't mean he sang quietly under his breath! You could hear him singing from down the block, and you came out to meet him. His singing was his calling card – he never knocked or rang the doorbell. His songs varied from Elvis to opera, but they were always upbeat. And he seemed to enjoy the smiles his singing brought to others as much as he enjoyed the singing itself.

The Singing Egg Man was an early role model for me of how **you can choose to do the things you do in a more people-oriented manner and when you do, everyone benefits…including you!**

My parents were also role models. They didn't spend a lot of time teaching my brother and me about respect, kindness or compassion. Instead, they taught us through their actions. They went about their everyday lives, all the while demonstrating how we ought to treat other people. My father knew the value of treating people with respect and was an exceptional builder of relationships. He never expected anything other than respect in return, and yet he received so much more: co-workers and friends helped him through difficult times; his wife and kids never wanted to disappoint him not because of intimidation but because of the respect and consideration he showed us.

Do your employees feel that way about you? Do they want to give discretionary effort because you respect them and treat them well? **Your attitudes and behaviors are the prime indicators of whether you will get compliance or commitment from your team. It's**

your choice – which do you want?

If you're still not convinced of the importance of the people side of business, you will likely never experience the full engagement your team will give when they feel you care about them. But perhaps you are a leader who believes there is a direct connection between people and profit but who keeps waiting for a "better time" to build relationships or coach your employees. Or maybe you think that treating people with decency and respect is simply the right thing to do, but you too easily get caught up in the busyness of life, just as we all do. If you're constantly saying to yourself that you'll focus on people issues when this project is done or that deadline is met, let me give you some advice: change the way you do the things you do, *now!* You'll have your employees singing your praises…

> *"You make my life so bright,*
> *You make me feel alright,*
> *The way you do the things you do."*
> *– The Temptations*

How *You* Doin'?

> ➤ Do you use your busy schedule as an excuse for not interacting on a personal level with your team members or taking the time to show them compassion and empathy?

> ➤ How do others in your circle react to you? Are you aware of the impact of your interpersonal skills (or lack thereof) on team and organizational results?

> ➤ Do you encourage or discourage those on your team who try to add a human touch to their interactions with others?

StreetSavvy Techniques

1. **Have a pleasant demeanor.** It doesn't take any more time to smile and make eye contact with people than it does to walk around with your head down or a scowl on your face. Stop thinking about your challenges and pressures long enough to acknowledge people. Oh, and by the way, I hear that cell phones can be surgically removed from ears for a very reasonable price!

2. **Respond sooner rather than later to requests for information or help.** If you're going to have to provide an answer anyway, why not do it as soon as possible? Chances are, the sooner you respond, the sooner that person can help *you* in return.

3. **Every time you communicate, force yourself to be aware of non-verbal signals.** Facial expressions, tone of voice and body language send a message about how much you do or don't care. When giving instructions or asking employees to take on a difficult task or additional work, include some recognition or positive feedback. This may take a few extra seconds (did you get that – not minutes or hours, *seconds*) but the payoff will far exceed the minimal investment of time. And remember to always add a pleasant "please" or "thank you" or similar comment to the beginning or end of any encounter with an employee.

Maybe you're thinking, "Why should I ask nicely or thank them? It's their job. I should be able to simply tell employees what to do." Let me ask you: How do *you* feel when someone – your boss, spouse, friend – tells you to do something and then doesn't thank you? And how does it feel when that same person asks with the addition of *one simple word* (please) or gives a simple two-word response (thank you)? That's what I thought. Enough said.

4. **Leverage your existing activities to build relationships with team members and co-workers.** When we were kids, one of our chores was to run errands for our parents. Since we walked everywhere we went, we developed the phrase, "Walk me." Fundamentally, it meant "walk with me." But ultimately, it came to mean much more. "Walking" each other provided companionship and allowed us to build relationships, all while getting our "job" done.

   My mom was a StreetSavvy woman. If she asked me to run an errand – like going to Aunt Minnie's house to pick up the brachiole – she'd quickly add, "Why don't you get Danny to walk you?" She knew that the companionship of a friend made the chore more palatable.

   The next time you're headed to the lunchroom or out to eat, ask a team member to "walk you." Take someone with you when you go to lunch, to get coffee or even to a conference. You're going anyway, and these are great opportunities to get to know people and build relationships.

   Likewise, take advantage of regular casual situations – in the break room, at lunch, before meetings – to role model high-touch behaviors like asking employees about their family members, hobbies, favorite sports teams, latest vacation, etc. Remember Mama Lucia's wisdom: relationships make the work more pleasant.

20

Fight City Hall...
Hold Leaders Accountable
All the Way Down the Line

Philadelphia in the 1950s and 60s was a city known for inefficiency and corruption. We didn't talk about it much except when someone asked, "Who do you know down at City Hall? My son got a parking ticket." Or a neighbor said, "My lazy nephew needs a job...there has to be a do-nothing job for him with the City." We heard these kinds of statements so often that it became normal to expect a certain level of corruption and ineptitude from our local politicians. So normal, in fact, that most citizens learned to operate within that framework. That's just the way things worked.

Philadelphia City Hall, 1949
Photo courtesy of PhillyHistory.org, a project of the Philadelphia Department of Records.

What we didn't realize was that something was definitely going on behind the scenes – something that created the problem and then allowed it to continue.

No, it wasn't backroom payoffs or blackmail, although I'm sure those things weren't uncommon. It was *a lack of leadership accountability.* Each bureaucrat had his own version of the excuse, "It's not my job." But even worse, it was perfectly acceptable to *not* hold others responsible for fulfilling the jobs they were being paid to do. Each leadership level at City Hall, starting at the very top, did not hold the level below it accountable. Eventually, the "it's-not-my-job" mentality and culture trickled down to the local politicians – the Committee Men, as they were called – who were supposed to handle issues at the neighborhood level like fixing streetlights and potholes.

Now, you might say that this same sad situation still exists in government today. Maybe it does, but that is a discussion for another day. Equally unfortunate is that this same lack of leadership accountability frequently exists in organizations that we would otherwise think of as "enlightened." I believe that most of today's leaders are not being held accountable for huge portions of their stated responsibilities – specifically, those associated with the people side of their jobs.

If I had only a moment in an interview to discuss factors that negatively impact almost every business, I would talk about the lack of leadership accountability pandemic. As leaders, we all too often do not hold the leaders below us accountable for the critical aspects of the people side of their job – things like recognition, coaching, feedback and communication. And the irony is that we would never accept this lack of performance in operational areas. Imagine a controller who doesn't understand or like working with numbers or a salesperson who refuses to talk with customers or close deals. How about an IT manager who's intimidated by technology? We wouldn't tolerate any of these situations for a minute. In fact, we likely wouldn't hire these people in the first place. And yet leaders across Corporate America ignore their people-based leadership responsibilities every day virtually without consequence.

Leaders who say that they "just aren't good" at the people side of business should be no more accepted and tolerated than a CFO who isn't good at accounting and finance.

Look, I realize this is strong stuff, but someone has to say it. I've just spent the last 19 chapters sharing techniques to help you and the other leaders in your organization do what needs to be done. But quite honestly, if no one is holding you accountable for quality leadership, you just wasted your time. It's that simple.

It all comes down to leadership accountability, and I'm here to tell you that accountability isn't happening for the most part in business today.

If you don't believe me, let me ask you this: How many CEOs are held accountable by their board or stockholders for achieving results *on the people side of their business*? We could probably count them on one hand! There aren't enough boards that truly hold their top executives responsible for financial goals, let alone people goals! Stories abound of CEOs earning big bonuses even when their company's bottom line is suffering and their stock is underperforming the market.

Now consider, if the CEO is not held accountable for people results, what is the likelihood that he/she will hold senior leadership responsible for people results? Slim to none. And if senior leadership isn't held accountable for the people side of business, you can bet middle management won't be either. Before you know it, the "people issues aren't my job" mentality and culture have trickled down all the way to front-line supervisors and managers. Sounds a lot like Philadelphia City Hall and the Committee Men of my youth!

Ideally, every leader in an organization, from the CEO to front-line supervisors, should focus on the people side of business. But in the real world – on the Corporate Streets – we both know that often doesn't happen. Sure, there's a lot of lip service paid to the people side of business, but those sentiments often don't hold true in the daily operations and actual culture of the organization.

Why is this lack of leadership accountability for people results so prevalent? For many of the same reasons that I've already talked about throughout this book.

First is the inherent difficulty of measuring results on the people side of business. While top executives often complain about the inability to measure soft skills, they think they can measure just about everything else and show a connection to the bottom line. But that's simply not true. Constantly upgraded technology, lavishly decorated offices and lobbies, corporate conferences and million-dollar travel budgets are just a sampling of initiatives and financial-statement line items for which it is virtually impossible to prove a return on investment. I'm not suggesting these expenses aren't important or valuable; I'm simply pointing out that you typically can't tie them directly to financial results. But just because you can't measure the ROI of something doesn't mean there isn't one.

Another reason for this lack of leadership accountability is a deep-down belief that people issues – engagement, retention, recognition, coaching, performance appraisal and the like – are nice, but not essential. Despite all the evidence to the contrary, many leaders still aren't convinced that people issues have enough direct impact on the bottom line to make them worth the price in time and money. So it's not surprising there is no accountability for people-based issues.

Hold Leaders Accountable All the Way Down the Line

The accountability issue is especially difficult to deal with because it lies beneath the surface and is rarely talked about or exposed – just like it was at City Hall. Those politicians knew they would not be kicked out of office for their nepotism and corruption. Likewise, **today's leaders know they won't lose their job for failing to deliver on the people issues, as long as they can deliver on the bottom line.**

What we need is a "sunshine law" to get the truth out in the open. Honest dialogue about the realities of leadership accountability for people initiatives is the first step. We must go beyond platitudes and treat the people in our organizations with the utmost care. When it comes right down to it, the only way to make that happen is to hold leaders responsible for people interactions in the same way they are held responsible for materials, processes and profits. Things will never really change – no matter how much money, resources, time and training we throw at the people side of business – until leaders, from the CEO to the front line, are held accountable.

My challenge to you is this: first and foremost, **hold *yourself* accountable for the people side of your job**. Regardless of what other leaders in the organization say or do with respect to the people side of business, you have an opportunity and a responsibility to get it right. If you are a leader of leaders, you are in a position to enhance or destroy leadership accountability. You have the tools to make it happen, from role modeling to performance appraisal. The truth is, you know what you need to do, you just need to do it. Just a few leaders can shift the culture of an entire organization. All it takes is a few leaders who are willing to make the choice to be people-focused leaders. Soon, your impressive results will encourage other leaders to shift their focus, and before long, you will have a critical mass of leaders dedicated to the people side of business.

There are those who will say that there are plenty of successful people who are not (or were not) held accountable for their actions. The politicians in Philadelphia, for example, who drove big cars and smoked even bigger cigars. Or the star athletes and celebrities who break the law or violate basic ethics and yet are more popular than ever. Aren't they successful without being accountable? I guess that depends on your definition of success.

How do you and your organization define success? Is success achieving a positive bottom line at any cost – generating profits at the expense of people? Or are the means just as important as the end results?

How you lead is directly tied to your beliefs about the value of people and the role they play in the organization's success. In fact, I'll go so far as to say that if you don't believe people are absolutely crucial to your organization's success, then maybe a leadership role is not for you.

There's an adage that you can identify people's priorities by looking at two things: their calendar and their checkbook. These two items will show you how they spend their time and their money. I believe you can similarly identify an organization's priorities by looking at where it spends its time and resources. As an organization, *how you doin'*? Do you spend your time and resources on profits alone or on profits and people?

If you will hold yourself and other leaders accountable for the people side of your business, you will reap plenty of rewards with both people and profits.

How *You* Doin'?

- As an individual leader, what do your calendar and "checkbook" look like? Do you spend your time and resources on profits alone or on profits and people?

- Do you hold *yourself* accountable for the people side of business, even if your boss doesn't?

- Do you solicit feedback from others (both above and below you) on how well you are doing with respect to your people responsibilities?

- If you are a leader of leaders, do you hire and promote individuals for their people skills as well as their technical skills? If not, *why not*?

StreetSavvy Techniques

The techniques for holding leaders accountable are actually quite simple, just as so many things on the streets are:

1. **Establish crystal-clear, concrete responsibilities and expectations with respect to the people side of business.** Then consistently and regularly communicate those to leaders and gain their commitment to follow them. Never forget that "stuff" rolls downhill – and down the line. Be cognizant of how expectations at upper management levels will translate to leaders way down the organizational chart on the front lines. Start with a few basic, reasonable expectations. After initial success, add more people-based expectations one at a time.

2. **Coach leaders who exhibit gaps between expected and actual performance on people issues.** Since there is a good chance this will be the first time they have been held accountable for

results on the people side of business, don't expect them to know there are gaps. Remember to practice patience. New habits take time to develop. It will likely take months or even years to truly build a culture of leadership accountability for the people side of your business.

3. **Recognize and reward leaders who get it right**. Publicly acknowledge accomplishments in meetings, emails, newsletters and on your intranet. Whenever possible, promote those leaders who achieve the greatest results on the people side of your business. More than likely, these same leaders will also produce the greatest operational results (no coincidence there). Public recognition also clarifies expectations by providing specific examples of the kind of behavior you are looking for.

4. **Actually hold leaders accountable**, up to and including termination if necessary. There's nothing like a real-life example to show where you stand on a subject. When other leaders understand that you are serious about people results, they will usually fall in line. Taking action to genuinely hold leaders accountable will have a greater impact on the organization than any speech about leadership ever could.

21

Remember Uncle Tony's Cigar Box... Sweat the Small Stuff

Growing up, I had an Uncle Tony. He wasn't actually an uncle; he was one of my dad's war buddies who didn't have a family. So we "adopted" him. In many respects, he was more of an uncle to me than some of my biological uncles. Like so many other men in the neighborhood, Uncle Tony was a short (about 5' 5"), bald Italian guy. He was little in stature, but big in heart.

My Uncle Tony.

One of the many things I remember about Uncle Tony was what he did for us kids at Christmastime. Everything about Christmas was exciting. But going to Uncle Tony's house for our annual Christmas party was extra special, and we looked forward to it for weeks beforehand. At some point during the party – when he perceived that we couldn't wait any longer – Uncle Tony would gather all of the kids around him in a circle. Then he'd bring out an old, faded yellow cigar box filled to the top with pennies, nickels, dimes and quarters.

As we fiddled anxiously, Uncle Tony invited each child, one by one, to put two hands into the cigar box and pull out as many coins as he/she could. Whatever we could hold in our hands was ours to keep. I can still remember how the coins felt cool to the touch and how much fun it was to run my fingers through them.

"Come on," he'd say, encouraging us, "get in there and get a big handful!" He'd stand there watching us with a look of pure joy on his face. When every child had reached into the box, we'd all yell, "Thank you, Uncle Tony!" Then it was a race to the kitchen table to count out the coins into little stacks to see who'd gotten the most.

By today's standards, Uncle Tony's cigar box may not sound like a big deal. But back then, for kids of somewhat modest means, it was huge! We usually got about $3.00, which was enough to go to a movie (with lots of popcorn and candy) or buy a year's supply of comic books or pimple balls.

Uncle Tony probably collected his spare change all year long to fill that cigar box. Just a little bit here and there. It wasn't a lot of money to him. But what was a small thing to him was huge to us and garnered our loyalty and endeared him to us for life. And I do mean for life – Uncle Tony carried on his Christmas tradition for at least 25 years and was still pulling out the faded yellow cigar box when my children were young.

There's something to be said for a memory that's as vivid years later as it was the day it happened.

I was reminded of Uncle Tony and his cigar box when a friend of mine, who is a dedicated manager, was commenting on some of the shortcomings of the company he works for. At one point, an exasperated, pleading look came over his face and he said, "And you know, it would be nice if they could just provide some decent coffee!"

Decent coffee – a small (perhaps even minute) thing for a multi-hundred-million-dollar company. But for my friend and his co-workers, the coffee had become a daily reminder of what they perceived as the organization's lack of empathy for its employees. That perception carried over and influenced their feelings about other issues like compensation, benefits, working environment, budgets and employees' worth in the eyes of upper management.

Organizations and their leaders often forget to sweat the small stuff – seemingly inconsequential situations that can have a significant and real effect on employees' attitudes, engagement and productivity, and therefore, organizational results. A chair that doesn't squeak, a copier that works more often than not, bottled water, nameplates with the employees' names spelled correctly, enough chairs in the conference room so that people don't have to sit on the floor during staff meetings…nothing earth shattering. Yet these are the very things that irritate otherwise productive employees – employees who don't expect major changes or expenditures, but who do expect to be provided with reasonable necessities and amenities. After all, should employees really have to purchase and bring their own light bulbs because the company can't get around to replacing them?

Perhaps none of these examples are true in your organization. But let me ask you: do your employees have to face an inquisition to get the necessary supplies and equipment to do their job? Is work flow cumbersome and complex? Is there enough privacy in their cubicles that they can hold conversations with customers and vendors? And what about the small *intangible* things that make a big difference to employees? Does anyone call to check on them if they are out sick? Does anyone ask about their vacation, their parents' health, their child's soccer game or the movie they saw last weekend?

Just like Uncle Tony's cigar box was a big deal to us, small things can make a big difference to employees. So, contrary to the popular book series, I'm telling you that you should sweat the small stuff. When you do, you will earn big returns. Sweating the small stuff creates win-win situations. Employees win with "better coffee" and you (and the organization) win by having more productive, engaged employees.

So here comes the obvious question: If taking care of the small stuff produces a big ROI, then why are so many small things ignored, left undone and taken for granted?

As usual, there is no single answer. One reason is lack of awareness – those who have the authority or the budget to make the little things happen don't know those little things are important to employees. Why? Because employees long ago gave up providing feedback to management. Wouldn't you do the same if day after day you saw the same situation remain unresolved even though it wouldn't take a lot of time or money to settle? (Think conference room chairs and light bulbs.)

Another factor is the widening gap between the "haves" (senior leadership) and the "have nots" (employees). When your day-to-day needs and wants are readily satisfied, it's easy to lose empathy for those who are lower on the organizational ladder. I still think about the executive who once told me he didn't provide coffee for his employees because "they should just go to Starbucks." Yeah sure…when a Starbucks coffee and a Danish cost half of what his typical employee was earning per hour after taxes and deductions! He might as well have said, "Let them eat cake!"

And finally, many leaders don't see a connection between, say, better coffee and a better bottom line. These are likely the leaders who don't believe there is a valid ROI for engaging employees or building a positive culture. But they are the same leaders who don't think twice about spending thousands of dollars on holiday parties, company picnics or Thanksgiving turkeys (and similar gifts) that many employees don't even want.

As the leader, it's up to you to fix as many of the "small things" as quickly as you can. In fact, do something to resolve some annoying situation *today*. Going forward, remember Uncle Tony and his cigar box, and remember to sweat the small stuff. In all likelihood, it won't take much effort or money, and you'll be paid back with engaged, dedicated, and dare I say, *happy* employees.

How *You* Doin'?

- Do you empathize with your employees when they are frustrated or distracted by minor obstacles, irritations and annoyances? Heck, do you even know which small things are big deals to them? When was the last time you asked your team members what gets under their skin?

- When someone makes a request or suggests a fix that wouldn't require much time or money, do you take action to make it happen? Or do you brush it off as "no big deal" and move on?

- Is there anything that bothers you that was small at one time but has now grown into a major source of irritation? Have you talked with your leader about it? (If you have and there's been no resolution, then this is a big clue as to your organization's level of empathy and bureaucracy.)

StreetSavvy Techniques

1. **Create your own "cigar box" – provide an annual budget for the small stuff.** It doesn't have to be a large amount, but enough that you can fulfill your commitment to take care of those little things that are important to your team. If you don't have the authority or the budget to resolve an issue or fix a problem, at least apply your influence with those who do. Go ahead…cash in on your credibility to help those below you on the organizational ladder who may not have as much "in the bank" with higher-level decision makers.

2. **Calculate the ROI for "small stuff" expenditures whenever possible.** For example, if your graphic designers, analysts and engineers have been begging for larger computer monitors as they toil for eight hours a day on small, outdated screens, compare the cost of larger monitors to the dollar value of increased productivity throughout your entire department that would result from having appropriate equipment. At a cost of a few hundred dollars each, I'll bet another cheesesteak that you'd see a substantial ROI.

3. **Take responsibility for identifying the small things that are big things for your team members.** Don't pass the buck by putting together a committee to collect information about workplace issues. And make certain you maintain a demeanor that encourages your team members to approach you with small issues. Otherwise, they may not "bother" you with such trivialities, and instead, complain about them among themselves, spreading discontent. When an employee does share a need with you, it provides an opportunity for two-way communication. You can ask questions, clarify the problem, discuss possible solutions and actively combat the "they don't listen to us" syndrome.

Chris Antone, managing partner with the national workplace law firm Jackson Lewis, thinks sweating the small stuff is so important he recommends leaders carry a small, spiral-bound notepad at all times to jot down issues and problems employees bring to their attention. (You remember what a notepad is – that thing you used back in the dark ages before you had a PDA.)

4. **Give team members your full attention.** This is a small thing that is definitely a big thing to employees. When team members approach you, stop what you're doing, turn off your cell phone, don't look at your watch and don't check your email. Give them your full, undivided attention.

Yo!
So Now You Think You Know Everything?

My Uncle Dom used to say, "Yo! I just taught you everything I know, and you still don't know anything!"

Back then, I thought he was making a joke at his own expense – that he really hadn't taught me anything at all. As an adult, I have a different perspective. I think what he was trying to say is that someone can teach you something, but until you actually *do* it, you haven't truly learned it. I think Uncle Dom was wiser than I gave him credit for. (Sorry, Uncle Dom, and thank you for your insight.)

So I'll say to you, "Yo! I just taught you everything I know about being a StreetSavvy Leader, and you still don't know anything!"

Please don't be offended. It's not a slam against you. I say it to make the same point Uncle Dom was trying to make. You may have read this entire book and evaluated yourself on every **How You Doin'?** question. You may have reviewed every **StreetSavvy Technique** and even thought about how you might implement them. You may well understand what it means to be a StreetSavvy Leader. But until you actually implement the techniques, until you actually practice StreetSavvy Leadership…do it…live it…experience it, you won't truly know what it means to be a StreetSavvy Leader. (And by the way, the same is true of any book, class or training program.)

It doesn't matter what you've learned – what matters is what you do.

So what can you *do* to become a more StreetSavvy Leader?

First, know that being a StreetSavvy Leader is not a binary, yes-or-no issue. It's an incremental approach – identifying one leadership challenge or people problem and making a positive impact on that situation. Then doing it again and again and again. It's about being better today than you were yesterday. StreetSavvy Leadership requires ongoing effort and an ongoing awareness about your attitudes, actions and behaviors.

Second, commit to investing in yourself in order to become a better leader. StreetSavvy Leaders make short-term investments of time and energy for lasting, long-term gains. They get real and focus on their people, knowing they will get sustainable results in return. That is the YROI.

Third, have courage. StreetSavvy Leadership takes guts. It's not always easy to do the right thing or to take action in difficult circumstances. But understand that being StreetSavvy is not about being a "tough guy" or "tough gal." It's about having the fortitude and conviction to say what needs to be said and to do what needs to be done.

Fourth, check your progress. Put a recurring reminder in your PDA every six months to go back to www.StreetSavvyLeader.com and take the free **StreetSavvy Leader Self-Assessment**. You should see evidence in your scores that you are becoming a more StreetSavvy Leader. Taking this assessment on a regular basis will also identify areas where there is still room for improvement. (And if you haven't yet taken the online assessment, do it now so you will have a baseline score for future reference.)

And finally, hold yourself accountable. That is one of the most crucial aspects of StreetSavvy Leadership. StreetSavvy Leaders don't make excuses. They hold themselves personally accountable every day, day in and day out. Paul Yost, Manager of Leadership Research for the Boeing Company once said: "The most successful leaders perform at that level not because of one or two great moments, but because of the hundreds of small decisions they make throughout the day."

My hope is that I have been accountable to you by perhaps causing you to think differently about some things and by providing practical ideas that you can implement immediately to deal with the real challenges and problems you're facing on the Corporate Streets.

I also hope that in searching my past for answers to today's problems, I've encouraged you to do the same. What a waste it is to ignore a lifetime of learning by only looking to current events to help us through difficult times. Take some time to examine *your* history and recapture lessons learned from your own life experiences. No matter what kind of street you grew up on – a big city thoroughfare, a quiet suburban street, a small town lane or a quiet country road – solutions to many of your life and leadership challenges are right there within you.

I congratulate you for taking on one of the most important responsibilities there is – the leadership of people – and I wish you the best. I hope one day to meet you on the Streets and to shake the hand of another StreetSavvy Leader.

StreetSavvy Glossary

Blind Spots – Those areas where you and your organization tend to be provincial without realizing it. These are the same areas that could benefit the most from some updated thinking.

Captain Communication – Your superhero alter ego and the champion of powerful and creative communication. Your mission: to eliminate tall stacks of copious memos and unnecessary emails; to creatively battle information overload and defeat employee disinterest; to use your leadership powers to shine the light on critical information that relates to and affects employees' jobs and responsibilities.

Cultural Mismatch – When an employee or team member possesses the technical skills to get the job done, but his/her attitude, work ethic or personal qualities and characteristics are not a fit with your culture. Employees who are cultural mismatches negatively affect the culture of the organization and have a negative impact on the bottom line.

Gang – Your team, department or organization. A group of people who share common values and priorities and who identify with one another as a result of their unique "brand."

How You Doin'? – A classic South Philly-ism that serves as a reminder to candidly assess how well you are performing individually as a leader and as an organization with respect to the people side of business.

INI – Immediately Noticeable Impact. When a specific situation, action or behavior has a direct, powerful, short-term effect on results (rather than a subtle and longer-term effect). Look for INI when you practice effective people skills.

Leadership Accountability – When every leader in an organization, from the CEO to front-line supervisors, focuses on and is held responsible for the people side of business.

Recognition – Treating people as worthwhile human beings.

Right Fit Leadership – Selecting candidates for leadership positions who have demonstrated leadership skills (rather than only technical skills) or have at least shown interest and potential.

Roof It – A call for leaders at all levels to practice zero-based prioritizing, in which they work with their teams to identify and focus on top priorities and then completely eliminate unproductive, wasteful, non-ROI activities. As in, "Select the best and roof the rest!"

StreetSavvy – Confident, candid and courageous. Able to say what needs to be said and do what needs to be done. Able to hold oneself accountable.

StreetSavvy Leader – A balanced, results-oriented leader who not only understands the real-world Corporate Streets, but can also successfully work and lead in those streets. A leader who is willing to acknowledge the truth about himself/herself and the organization in order to **get real** and **get results**.

StreetSavvy Leadership – A proven style of leadership that allows you to hold people accountable and deliver results without compromising your values or being a jerk. Practical strategies and techniques (rather than platitudes and theories) for dealing with real-world challenges and problems, which can be implemented immediately and used every day.

Street Specialists –Team members who are "right fit" – whose technical and people skills are a match for their job responsibilities.

The Small Stuff – Seemingly inconsequential situations that can have a negative significant and real effect on employees' attitudes, engagement and productivity, and therefore, organizational results. Organizations and their leaders often forget to "sweat the small stuff."

The Way You Do the Things You Do – Combining or piggybacking people-focused activities with the operational activities you are already doing (rather than seeing them as add-ons). Produces higher returns for the *same* amount of time invested.

Trade Your Rags for Pots and Pans – The concept of getting rid of your old attitudes, thoughts and processes, and exchanging them for new ones that will likely be far more valuable and beneficial.

YROI – Your Return on Investment. What's in it for you – what *you* personally (not the organization) will get in return for your investment of time, energy and resources in becoming a StreetSavvy Leader.

South Phillyisms

Agida – Italian for "upset stomach," a condition made far more dramatic by making a pained face and moving your hand rapidly around your mid-section to show where it hurt.

Beeries – Beer and soda bottle caps used primarily to play a game called Dead Box. Also used as "buttons" and accessories for homemade scooters.

Birthday Punches – The punches on the arm your friends were allowed to give you on that special day, one for each year plus a final, really hard one for good luck.

Broad Street Bullies – The nickname given to the Philadelphia Flyers National Hockey League team, well earned in a city that had more than its share of bullies.

Butcher Shop Ladies – South Philly women who congregated at the local butcher shops and weren't afraid to tell it like it was. They had a great deal of influence with the other women in the neighborhood. They all dressed similarly – typically a housecoat with brightly colored flowers, no matter the time of year.

Cheesesteaks – Thinly sliced steak, cheese and cooked onions on a crusted roll. Made first and best in Philly. Probably one of the first foods thought of when the phrase "to die for" was coined.

Chips – As in, "I call chips on the ball." This meant that as the owner of the ball (or other piece of sports equipment), you would be reimbursed for its cost by anyone who roofed it or sent it down the gutter.

"Climb in My Window" – Request made by elderly neighbors on our street who frequently locked themselves out of their houses. An example of generations working together.

"Cross Me" – Request made by kids of adults (even strangers) to hold their hand or help them cross the street. One of the many small ways different generations helped each other.

Dead Box – A game played with beeries (bottle caps). Chalk boxes drawn on the street and you flicked your beerie from box to box until you reached the "dead box" and were poison. You then could hit other kids' beeries and knock them out of the game.

"Fugettaboutit!" – South Philly for "Forget it" or "Don't worry about it" or "No problem" or "No way that will happen!" Meaning depended on the emphasis and tone of voice.

Gravy – What true Italians call red sauce, as in, "Give me more gravy for my spaghetti."

Hairy Eyeball – The squinty-eyed, furrowed-brow, disapproving look you give someone when you want them to know you are not happy with their behavior.

Halfball – 1. A piece of sports equipment created by cutting a rubber ball (see **Pimple Ball**) in half with a pocket knife. 2. A popular street game involving pitching and hitting a halfball with a bat or sawed-off broom handle.

"How You Doin'?" – One of those great Philly-isms that is the general equivalent of "Wazup?"

"Hunks" – A term used to stake a claim to a piece or "hunk" of someone else's candy. Similar to calling "Shotgun!" to proclaim your right to sit in the front passenger seat of the car.

Javella Water – Laundry detergent sold in gallon jugs and delivered to your house. Cheaper than Tide or Oxydol, and the fact that it sounded Italian made it, of course, better!

La Famiglia – Italian for "the family."

Mooners – The proper way to pitch a halfball: underhand with the full "moon" side toward the batter. (Floaters – The incorrect way to pitch a halfball: with the cut, open side of the ball parallel to the ground making it harder to hit.)

Pimple Ball – A rubber ball similar in size to a tennis ball. Used to play many street games until it cracked or deflated (see **Halfball**).

Rag Man – A roaming street vendor who provided a tremendous service: the opportunity to swap your old, worn-out stuff for new stuff, specifically your old rags for new pots and pans.

Roof It – To forever lose or get rid of something (accidentally or intentionally) by throwing it on top of the flat roofs of the row houses in South Philly.

Singing Egg Man – A roaming street vendor who sold eggs and sang to draw customers out into the streets. A role model of how you can choose to do the things you do in a more people-oriented manner.

Spaghetti – Not the food, but the markings on the wall of Francis Scott Key Elementary School where we played Halfball that indicated whether a hit was a single, double, triple or home run.

Uncle Tony's Cigar Box – 1. An old, yellow cigar box used to collect spare change. 2. The annual Christmas tradition in which Uncle Tony let us kids grab and keep a handful of coins from the cigar box. A small thing to Uncle Tony, but a huge deal to us.

"Walk Me" – A request for someone to take a walk with you. To accompany a friend on an errand, as in, "I have to go to the store for my mom…walk me."

"Yo" – 1. A South Philly all-purpose greeting. 2. An exclamation that indicates irritation like when someone steps on your newly polished shoes.

Youse – South Philly for "several people," as in, "Youse guys know where I can get a good cheesesteak?"

Acknowledgements

The subject matter of this book encompasses my entire life's experiences as a leader, trainer, consultant, speaker and author. As a result, there are more people to acknowledge than could ever be listed here. So let me say thank you to all of the people over the years who lent me their wisdom, support and counsel, and who influenced my ideas, philosophies, methods and processes about leadership and the people side of business. Special thanks to the **ADL Associates**, a group of professionals who continually enhance my knowledge base and multiply my effectiveness with clients.

And of course, I could not have written this book without the many family members, friends, teachers, coaches, neighbors and other folks who played such a crucial role in my youth. My heartfelt appreciation goes out to all of you for the indelible mark you made on my life and my values, principles and beliefs. I am proud to be from South Philly!

There are some people who must be directly acknowledged for their contributions to this book: **Juli Baldwin,** who has re-defined the term Creative Editor during this project and whom I now refer to as "Essential Editor"! **Richard Lucia,** my brother, who has been with me through everything in life, including this project. **Melissa Monogue,** graphic designer extraordinaire, who took the South Philly street I grew up on and turned it into a book cover. And **Katie Booth,** who matched Melissa's creativity for the inside treatment. Friend and colleague **Brian Gareau** who helps me in just about everything I do these days. **Dan Salvano** who helped me remember the South Philly details. **Steve Ventura** who can be counted on to add value to my writing…every time. **Nicole Sanseverino** who lent her creative insights and provided a fresh, New-Millennial viewpoint. **Trey Sanseverino,** a young and effective illustrator. And **Pamela Work** for her keen attention to detail.

And last but certainly not least, thank you to my wife, **Michele Lucia,** who supports me in ways that make projects like this possible.

About the Author

THEN　　　　　　　　　　　**NOW**

Al Lucia has spent more than 30 years helping organizations and their leaders make the connection between value-driven practices and bottom-line results. As a consultant, speaker, coach and author, he has helped organizations of all types and sizes build employee commitment, match actions to values, improve overall performance and achieve better results. And as an experienced practitioner, he offers real-world solutions to today's most pressing business challenges.

He is the founder of ADL Associates, Inc., a nationwide network of **speakers, consultants and trainers** dedicated to providing business executives with customized solutions to today's people challenges. Known as **America's Lifeline to the People Side of Business**, Al stays in constant touch with emerging trends in leading companies across the nation, enabling his clients to learn from and adopt "the best of the best" business strategies.

Al's reputation as a lively, entertaining and engaging presenter is well earned. He is a popular and sought-after speaker, enhancing corporate events and national association conferences across the country. In addition, he founded and sponsors the annual HR Executive Forum with senior executives from Fortune 500 companies and other major corporations.

Al's client list is extensive and includes such notable organizations as GE, Wal-Mart, FedEx, Exxon-Mobil, Southwest Airlines, Home Depot, OfficeMax, Gaylord Hotels, Anthem Blue Cross Blue Shield, Bank of America, Caterpillar, National Semi-Conductor, Securitas, Con-Way Transportation, Ocean Spray, American Red Cross, Lakeland Electric and the Orlando Magic.

He has co-authored nine books, including the very successful *Leadership Secrets of Santa Claus*, as well as *A Slice of Life, Employee Commitment, Back to Basics*, the Jukebox Journey to Success series and three books in the popular Walk the Talk series. Articles by Al have been published in dozens of leadership, management and human resource periodicals.

StreetSavvy Leadership: Get Real. Get Results.

Whether through dynamic keynote presentations, interactive workshops or focused roundtable discussions, Al Lucia brings a truly unique blend of knowledge, energy and StreetSavvy experience to the subject of leadership. While there are many presenters who can competently address the topic of leadership, few can match Al's total package of experience, communication skills, credibility and humor. He is a true "category of one." Known as a "lifeline" to executives throughout the United States, Al's expertise comes not only from his life experiences growing up in South Philadelphia, but also from best practices and his work with some of America's most respected organizations.

In his thought-provoking **StreetSavvy Leadership** presentations, leaders at all levels learn proven, practical ways for dealing with real-world business challenges such as: employee engagement, workforce retention, generational differences and work-life balance. Al engages participants by asking, "How you doin'?" as only he can and then guiding them to identify strategies and solutions that will work every day. In a profound exercise, he also invites participants to examine their own "history" and life experiences to identify their own solutions to life and leadership challenges.

Al has shared his important yet entertaining message with scores of notable organizations, including Wal-Mart, Caterpillar, OfficeMax, Exxon Mobile, Scottish Rite Hospital, The American Red Cross, Gerdeau Ameristeel, The University of Texas and Gaylord Hotels. In addition, he has presented his practical approaches to "the people side of business" at conferences for associations such as The Society for Human Resource Management, The American Society for Training and Development and Meeting Professionals International.

Al's presentations can be delivered in various formats, from 45-minute keynotes to half- or full-day workshops. His other popular high-impact presentations include:

- **Taking HR To The Bottom Line**
- **Why Bother To Be Engaged?**
- **Employee Commitment: If You Build it Results Will Come**

To book Al Lucia for your next conference or in-house event, contact us at:
ADL Associates, Inc.
www.ADLassociates.com
al@ADLassociates.com
972-662-3068

Solutions for the People Side of Business

ADL ASSOCIATES, INC.

ADL Associates, Inc. is dedicated to providing business executives with customized solutions to today's people challenges. Experts on the People Side of Business, we are a nationwide network of **consultants, trainers, speakers and authors** with extensive practical experience and a high level of integrity. From individual employee challenges to overall leadership issues, we have the experts you need to produce the best outcomes.

Our associates have hundreds of years of combined experience in the business world and have worked with every type of organization across all industries, including over 400 of the Fortune 500. The expertise and services represented by the ADL Associates are diverse, covering more than 60 topics and concepts. You can rest assured that founder and principal Al Lucia *personally knows, respects and trusts each associate*. We guarantee their success in delivering results that will meet or exceed your expectations.

ADL Associates is committed to making a positive difference in the organizations we serve. Our business solutions include:

- **Keynote Speakers** who inspire and motivate;
- **Trainers and Presenters** that effectively develop skills in all areas of professional and personal development;
- **Consultants** that deliver a return on investment with projects and processes;
- **Tools**, including books and videos, available through our on-line book store;
- **Hundreds of free on-line resources** – articles and free tips on a comprehensive list of topics that can easily be used in your company newsletters or shared with team members;
- A **Forum for HR Executives** to network and share best practices.

Let us save you time and headaches – contact us today to learn more about how our professionals can help your organization move to the next level. We are available to visit with you to analyze your specific needs and provide customized solutions.

ADL Associates, Inc.
www.ADLassociates.com
al@ADLassociates.com
972-662-3068
1111 Holy Grail Drive
Lewisville, Texas 75056

Four easy ways to order!

The StreetSavvy Leader
Get Real. Get Results.

PHONE
Call 972.662.3068
Monday–Friday, 8:30 AM – 5:00 PM CST

WEBSITE
Visit us on-line 24 hours a day at
www.ADLassociates.com

MAIL
ADL Associates
1111 Holy Grail Drive
Lewisville, TX 75056

FAX
972.662.0978